VISITING LIFE

VISITING LIFE

WOMEN | TIME | OUTSIDE
DOING | ON THE

BRIDGET KINSELLA

HARMONY BOOKS
NEW YORK

Published in the United States by Harmony Books, an imprint of the
Crown Publishing Group, a division of Random House, Inc., New York.

www.crownpublishing.com

HARMONY BOOKS is a registered trademark and the Harmony Books
colophon is a trademark of Random House, Inc.

Library of Congress Cataloging-in-Publication Data
Kinsella, Bridget.
Visiting life : women doing time on the outside / Bridget Kinsella.—1st ed.
p. cm.
1. Prisoners—Family relationships—California.   2. Man-woman
relationships—California.   3. Kinsella, Bridget.   I. Title.
HV8886.U5K56 2007
362.82'92—dc22   2006038268

ISBN 978-0-307-33836-5

Printed in the United States of America

Design by Lauren Dong

10 9 8 7 6 5 4 3 2 1

First Edition

For my great big Italian-Irish family,
who I take with me everywhere

Contents

CHAPTER 1

JUST VISITING

The first time I walked into a maximum-security prison I dressed like a lawyer—though it wasn't my intention. Let's just say there are lots of rules about what a woman can and cannot wear inside a men's maximum-security prison: no inmate-blue denim and no cop-green khaki seemed the most important ones. I figured it best to have a modest hemline and thought to-the-knee was plenty modest. The guard didn't agree and sent me back to my car to change.

The last time I'd changed clothes in my car was the summer I worked two jobs and went to night school. Somewhere stopped in traffic along the New Jersey Turnpike between my job at Six Flags Great Adventure in Jackson and class at Rutgers University in New Brunswick, I decided to wiggle out of my work skirt and into my student cutoffs without looking to see if there were any truckers who might get an eyeful. This time I am more conscious of changing in the open as I shimmy out of my pale green dress deemed inappropriate and into a black-and-white number I think will pass prison scrutiny.

How did I get here? I ask myself, scanning the myriad fences, razor wire, and looming guard towers of Pelican Bay State

Prison. Yes, Pelican Bay. Whenever anyone writes or speaks of this notorious prison in Crescent City, California, they usually call it "the worst of the worst." They mean the worst criminals and the worst treatment.

I think back on my twenty-something self cruising along in my white-with-red-vinyl-roof Pontiac Sunbird as my thirty-nine-year-old self changes shoes in my rust-colored Chevy Cavalier not much bigger than my beloved first set of wheels. The older I get the more I realize we never actually shake off the internal image of our younger selves but hopefully evolve from it. Out of about three hundred students in high school I graduated something like thirteenth (just my luck). At the top but not *the* top—A minus—because Mrs. Bliss was right: things came too easily to me and I didn't always apply myself. Nonetheless, I displayed all the trappings of a young woman ready to make her mark. Cheerleader. Yearbook editor. The dutiful youngest daughter of five in a loving Irish-Italian working-class family putting herself through school. Girls like me don't grow up to visit convicted murderers in maximum-security prisons.

Yet here I am.

" 'Twas reading that did me in," I say out loud as if I'm spinnin' a yarn for some imaginary person in the passenger seat now littered with discarded clothes. I laugh because after eight years of living alone, much of that time spent working at home, I notice that I talk to myself a lot.

As I step out of the car I do think I look like a lawyer. I assume that I am a very different sort of person than the other people visiting today, but I cannot put my finger on why I think that way. I wear black patent leather high-heeled Mary Janes, a pleated dress dangling just below the knee, a black blazer that covers me from shoulder to midthigh. All I need to complete the effect is a briefcase. Instead, I clutch the plastic Ziploc bag containing the only things I am allowed to bring into the big house: thirty one-dollar bills (which the prisoner is never allowed to touch), some old pictures, and my car keys.

How did I get here?

It's simple, really. For ten years I worked as a journalist covering the publishing world. Then a year ago I tried my hand at being a literary agent. It made sense. I had earned a reputation as someone who could judge the commercial or literary viability of a book. Why not do it from the other side?

Once you head down that road, manuscripts appear from the strangest sources. Seems like everyone has an uncle or a friend or a spouse who wrote a book and just needs someone to help them get it published. One of my friends is a writer who taught creative writing at Pelican Bay.

He assured me that each week during his class the other inmates would read first, saving the star student's latest installment for last as if it were dessert. Although my friend wanted me to read his student's book, he was reluctant to give a woman's name to a convicted murderer doing life without parole, plus fifteen. Besides, he wasn't supposed to help a convict with any potential commercial enterprise. Instead, he hinted to his student, CDC#K78728, that he might send the unfinished manuscript to his own publisher in New York. When the publisher rejected the manuscript, he forwarded it on to me. The inmate's letter to the publisher included these postscripts: "I am currently incarcerated in Pelican Bay State Prison. This will cause a slight delay in our written correspondence. P.P.S. Life sentence. Murder. And if you have any more questions, feel free to ask me."

The book blew me away. Snap! From the first page it took off and barreled its way along to a shocking conclusion. I decided to contact this Rory Mehan and tell him I thought he was a talented writer. At the very least I knew I'd make his day. Knowing it's not smart to give your real address to a man in prison, I got myself a private mailbox address just in case (Of what? That he'd break out of prison?) and sent off the letter: "Dear Mr. Mehan, blah, blah, blah. Talented writer. Send me more. Oh, and keep writing. Sincerely, Bridget Kinsella, Literary Agent." I didn't mention murder.

A month later I found a white envelope with my name and address written in a small-cap penciled print in my mailbox. I opened it in my car. There was no salutation, no "dear so-and-so," it just took off. Much like the novel he wrote. My first real glimpse of Mr. Mehan came on three-hole-ring-punched, school-ruled paper:

> So I'm sitting here in my concrete box, just looking out my tiny sliver of a window, amazed at what I see. Ash is falling from the miscolored afternoon sky in thick swirling flurries like snow, like dead grey skin falling from a psoriatic finally giving in to the constant promising pleasure of the itch.
>
> And the television tells me that 32,000 fires are currently blazing across America. Oregon, eight miles away, is not the only state burning.
>
> And the ash, it just keeps falling, filling a foreign orange world, fluttering down from a steadily purpling sky, a fresh bruise growing darker right before my eyes. It clings to the stinging razor wire. It piles up in drifts.
>
> It's the middle of the summer.
>
> I haven't seen the sun in weeks.
>
> And thousands of dead squid are washing ashore in

California, littering the postcard beaches, disrupting the fantasy/delusion that everything is all-right. The newscaster says that "nobody knows why."

I'm laughing.

It's my new way of crying.

Because I'm thinking if thousands of dead squid covering California beaches is not a natural occurrence, then isn't it obvious that <u>we</u> [underlined three times] are the reason why?

And that, Bridget Kinsella, is when your letter slides under my cell door, skidding across the smooth stone floor to land inches from my right hush puppy.

Murderer or not, the man knows how to make an entrance. Nearly a year and many letters later, here I am visiting my client at Pelican Bay.

The guard approves of my change of clothes. I fill out a form with Rory's California Department of Corrections (CDC) number on it, my name and address and relationship to the prisoner. I write "friend," because we are friends by now, having written to each other for months, and it is no business of the prison if I am his literary agent. The guard, a pleasant man with close-cropped hair and a well-ironed uniform, processes the paperwork to make sure I am an "approved" visitor. Since it took awhile for me to change clothes, I am the only person left in the visiting way station. It's not much to look at. It could almost be a small-town post office. I am fascinated by a glass-encased display with T-shirts and sweatshirts sporting the Pelican Bay logo as if it's some sort of sports franchise to cheer on. Someone with an odd sense of humor came up with the slogans for the shirts. "Felony Day Camp" is my favorite.

I am nervous, but I am not sure why. There are several guards behind the counter, a handful of men and one woman. The guard who asked me to change clothes calls my name. I walk forward and another guard tells me I almost look too good to be going in there—but he says it with a smile, as a way to ease my nerves. He instructs me to take off my shoes, jewelry, or anything else that might set off the metal detector to my right. Even though it's summer, the linoleum feels cold and the carpeted hump comes as a relief when I step into the machine. That is, until the alarm sounds and I have to turn back.

"Underwire?" asks the second guard. "Yes," I answer, a little flushed because no one likes setting off an alarm. He hands me scissors with the tips chopped off and tells me to go into the ladies' room to cut them out. "But this is my favorite bra," I half joke. "Can't I just take it off?" That elicits a resounding "no" from both guards. So I go to the ladies' room and do as I'm told. The second button comes off of my dress when I remove it to get to my pretty pink bra that is about to become wireless. Cutting silk—even faux silk—with sawed-off scissors isn't easy, but I manage. My jacket covers my dress so I just button up as best I can. I return to the desk and hand my dress button to the guard to hold for me.

The alarm goes off again. I can't imagine why. I have never had such trouble in airports—and that's with the underwire. The guard asks me what I am wearing under my dress. "Panty hose," I say, "underwear. That's it." He tells me that next time I should wear a slip. Still flushed from the alarm, I'm thinking that I don't even own a slip, and then the other guard discovers the culprit. My button. It's cloth over metal. Who knew? I have nothing else to change into and I hope they are not going to send me to the "hospitality" house and make me borrow some unknown woman's donated clothes.

This is not helping my nerves. Then the guards do something really nice. They let me walk around the metal detector where they wand me and then lead me into a small room. A guard hands me my belongings in a scuffed-up, wooden "in-box" kind of container. I hastily put on my shoes and jewelry. One guard stamps the underside of my wrist with something that doesn't show in normal light and the other buzzes the door open.

I gingerly walk through the door leading out the back of the building and enter the first of two fenced-in pens I must cross to get beyond the prison's carefully constructed and lethal fences. I jump a little bit at the sound of a gate mechanically opening before me. A sign tells me not to approach the gate until it is fully opened. I comply and walk through and enter the second fence-and-concrete pen. Three concentric fences snaking around the prison complex stretch out on either side of the pen. The first and the third fences look like normal Home Depot chain-link— although they stand about twenty feet in the air and have razor wire looped at the top. I'm guessing that the middle fence, composed of a delicate, spiderweb-like wire connected to metal braces every few feet, is electric, and I don't dare touch anything. I hear the gate closing behind me. The gate I face doesn't begin to open until the other one completes its journey.

When I step out of the second pen and onto a walkway I think that I am now on "the inside." But that's just silly. The visiting buildings are down a concrete path and about twenty-five yards away. I assume they are separate from the general population and supermax buildings and heavily guarded. I take a deep breath and start walking. The California sun blazes down on me and I notice that the walkway is unadorned with any vegetation. I hear someone tapping on one of those sliver windows in the two-story concrete bunker of a building to my left. My heels clack against the sidewalk as I quicken my pace. There is nothing much to look at as I pass through an unnatural courtyard of concrete and dirt into a gray, nondescript one-story building. Mostly it feels like I am walking into a school, and I remember that the public high school in the town where I attended Catholic school was actually designed by an architect who specialized in prisons. It had slits for windows, too.

Inside there are two reception areas, one to my left and one to my right. I turn left as told. The guard seated at a desk in front of a closed-circuit monitor looks at my pass and takes my ID. On his belt there are huge keys, of the size and shape that might open some medieval castle. I comment on this and the guard says the kids love those keys as he uses one to open the door into the visiting room for me.

Then I'm standing inside a sterile room. If not for the fact that all the prisoners wear denim shirts and jeans, the setting feels almost like a normal cafeteria. With armed guards, that is. There are vending machines, small round tables, and unforgiving fluorescent lights. A guard at a slightly elevated counter across the room motions to me. Briskly I walk past the several groups of people in midvisit. A little girl of about three catches my eye. Audrey Hepburn getting ready to visit Sing Sing in *Breakfast at Tiffany's* comes to mind, as she says to George Peppard: "You think it should be sad seeing children there; but it isn't. They're all dressed up with ribbons in their hair." This girl is all dressed up with no ribbons but several braids with pink fasteners adorning her head.

The guard says, "Over here." He takes my pass and briefs me on procedures.

"There is a brief kiss and embrace allowed at the beginning and end of the visit," he tells me sternly but through a buck-toothed smile. I tell him it's not *that* kind of visit. "You have no idea what I see up here," he continues. The smile is innocuous enough, but I'm wondering if maybe this guy likes watching such exchanges just a little too much.

All the other guards have been so friendly. Believe me: I am happy for their presence. I am glad they care what I look like coming in here, because while I wanted to look pretty for the visit—as I would for any business or social meeting—I am well aware that I am in a room with men who do not see very many women. And while I am not in the least afraid of meeting Rory, I am a little afraid of these other guys. I am even more conscious of that in here than I would be on a New York City subway at midnight.

The guard, whom I am already mentally nicknaming "Buck Tooth," assigns me a table with the number "16" stenciled on it. He tells me that during the visit we are only allowed to hold hands—on *top* of the table. I fight the urge to snap at him and admit to myself that I wouldn't last a week in prison.

Even though I wrote to tell Rory weeks ago that I was coming to visit, the letter somehow got lost in the system. Buck Tooth comes over to my table and says it might take awhile because Rory was at work and went back to his tier to take a shower. He doesn't use Rory's name—first or last. The smile kills me because I can tell he is the one in the bunch like Officer Percy Wetmore in *The Green Mile:* He's drunk with power and he hates these guys. He hates even more that we visit. These are my assumptions, anyway. His eyes linger on my legs as he walks away.

No matter, I tell myself, and go get a cup of coffee from the vending machine. I pass the next half hour trying not to stare at anyone. No one has told me how to act, though it is not fear that keeps me from looking so much as it is an unspoken code of respect. Respect is everything in prison.

Of course I can't help but look at the others in the antiseptic room. There is a bespectacled Asian man joined with his family gathered around their small table. He looks nineteen and as if he could easily pass for a sophomore at some engineering school. They are playing cards. The black woman waiting next to me passes the time with a children's coloring book. One couple makes popcorn in one of two microwaves at either side of the guard's desk.

Finally the heavy door near the vending machines opens and three men head straight to Buck Tooth at the counter. Then they make their way toward their visitors. No Rory. Out of the corner of my eye I watch an African American couple kiss. It's a pretty passionate kiss and I can see their tongues touching even though I am trying not to look. Well, I am trying not to be caught looking, anyway.

I notice that a couple of the men have "CDC Prisoner" written in big yellow letters down one of their pant legs and across the back of their shirts. I hope Rory isn't wearing something like that.

More time passes. A young blond man and an older blond woman who I think is his mother go out onto the patio where there are three concrete picnic tables. I watch hand-holding couples walk in circles outside, always in the same counterclockwise direction.

A buzzer sounds and the corrections officer who is talking with Buck Tooth leaves the counter and goes through the heavy door. He has those medieval skeleton keys, too. A few minutes later two men come into the room. Rory? I cannot be sure because he does not look at me and so I cannot match him to the picture he sent.

But when he turns from the counter to walk toward me I know it's him. He's beaming. He's smaller than I had expected, but pumped. His muscles are obvious even beneath his prison blues. No "CDC Prisoner" label marks him. I get up and he gives me a great big hug, just as he had warned me he would in his last letter. With my heels on I stand about two inches shorter than Rory, so I figure he's about five foot eight.

In the ten months since we began writing we have exchanged fourteen letters and one Christmas card. At first we stuck mostly to the topic of writing but then gradually we began to share our stories with each other, and I even let him call me a few times before this in-person meeting, so we had a good idea what we'd be like. But seeing me for the first time, the person he called his "rainbow in the dark" for encouraging his writing, obviously makes him shy, and I can see him struggle for words.

"I can't believe you're here," he says as we sit down.

"I wrote to tell you, but I guess you didn't get the letter yet," I say. Prison mail often takes three or four weeks.

"I don't care, this is great." I can tell he is trying to sound calm. He's embarrassed because he didn't have time to shave. "I wanted to get out here as soon as I could." He smiles crookedly and rubs the slight stubble around a goatee.

I show Rory the thirty dollars in my Ziploc bag for the vending machines, but he is too nervous or excited to eat anything. (It's mostly crap, anyway.) You are allowed to bring in ten photographs. The numbers are arbitrary—a form of power— and so I brought in eleven. The guard in the processing center paused as he counted them, but he let it go. "I'll show you the pictures later," I say, but when I tell Rory about my tiny act of defiance a slightly mocking smile lightens his expression and he relaxes.

He turned thirty in April. He's been incarcerated since he was nineteen. Murder. I asked him about it in my third letter. When I decided to work with Rory and to become his friend, I grappled quite a lot with how I felt about his crime. I do not dismiss it. I do not condone it. I pray for the victim and his family. Rory is serving his time, though, and I am not his judge. I tell myself that a man is not made of one single action, great or small, horrific or noble, but of his lifetime of action—or inaction, for that matter.

He tells me that a part of him has stayed nineteen, stunted at his sentencing hearing. In subsequent visits I will learn more about what Rory did; for now, I am satisfied with what he has told me and what I asked a journalist friend to uncover. When you know someone in prison it is sometimes best not to have all the facts.

When he answered my third letter, he included a copy of a Polaroid picture of himself holding his baby niece. To be seen as human, I think. He wrote:

> *And, oh, by the way, to answer your question . . . I was nineteen years old. I was dealing, using, getting high off my own supply. I was up for 28 days. My friend was killed in a drug deal. I was enraged. I was insane. And I think the term I'm looking for is 'drug psychosis,' but the judge disagreed. [Here he drew his own personal version of a smiley face.] So what I thought was righteous revenge, eye for an eye, was really just first degree murder and I was convicted of*

committing it on a teenage boy a few years younger than I was at the time.

And the funny thing is, which by funny I mean terribly sad, is that I deserve this! I was a bad person. I did the worst thing.

Bridget Kinsella [he likes writing my name], the truth is that I would give my own life to take it back, to make it right, believe me when I say that [underlined twice] is a given. But no one wants to hear it and it does not change the fact that I will die in prison.

Still, I am determined to rise above my poor education, my bad choices, beyond the cold grey walls and the elec- trified death fences, far away from the violence which sur- rounds me . . . Because even though I may have done what they say I did, I am not who they say I am. Not anymore.

This first visit we do not talk about his crime much. I prefer to talk about his upbringing because there's always a backstory.

Rory says his parents got married when he was not quite two. He describes his father and his whole family on both sides as "Irish drunks." His father abandoned his mother in the hospi- tal with a broken pelvis after she had just given birth to their sec- ond child, Rory's sister. His mother worked hard to give the children everything she could—even private schooling. She had a hard time being alone, though, and took up with several abu- sive men. The men beat her in front of the children. One tried to strangle her with a telephone cord. She drank, too. But then she found God and everything changed.

"We were doing just fine without Him," says Rory.

His mother started getting upset with *his* sinful ways. He was twelve. She trashed his records and posters of pretty girls and beat him sometimes with a cutting board decorated with Bible verses.

As I listen I think that just about any person trusted to care for Rory abused him—with the exception of his Nana, for whom he learned to play the saxophone, her favorite instrument.

His story continues. At thirteen, he ran away and fell in with a bunch of teenage drug dealers not that far from where his mother lived in Sonoma County. His father lived nearby. Neither came looking for him. He managed to stay in school until he was sixteen and then he earned an equivalency diploma.

Hungry for love, he fell fast for a pretty girl named Amy, who had long black hair down her back. At around fifteen or sixteen (Rory admits that remembering the timing of his life is a little sketchy), he was already sexually active, drinking, using, and dealing drugs. But Amy introduced him to the needle. Then she rejected him when her former boyfriend (one of Rory's best friends) was released from jail. It crushed Rory, but he forced himself to move on. He sobered up, took his ill-gotten money, and went to Reno to attend culinary school.

"I make an amazing linguine with clam sauce," he brags to me. I don't have the heart to tell him I hate clams.

He had managed to start over, but after a few months in school he got a desperate call from Amy. Apparently, her boyfriend was killed in a drug deal. Rory went into a rage, got back on drugs, and used his gun.

I decide that that's enough for one visit and suggest we go sit outside.

We pick a concrete picnic table of our own and then it's my turn to share. I open the Ziploc bag and take out the pictures and place them facedown. I start with my mother, an Italian beauty. I do this on purpose because despite the Irish drunks in his family he is rather proud of his almost 100 percent Celtic blood. (There is a drop of Native American.) Also, it's obvious that Rory likes my Irish looks and I am not sure how I feel about that. But I want him to know who I am and my mother is the best place to start. I think I want to show him what a "normal," happy childhood looks like—not to shove it in his face, but to let him know it can exist.

With the sunlight streaming down on us, my blue eyes sparkle and shine when I talk about my Italian mom, whom I call without exaggeration "the personification of love." I can feel him looking deep inside of me as I continue with the picture show. I turn over the next photo, a miniature shot of me in first grade, wearing my school uniform with the tie askew. With my brown/auburn hair done up in Cindy Brady curls, I am as adorable as any seven-year-old with her two front teeth missing. He holds the little picture in his hand and stares at it. Then he stares at me.

"Your mother may be Italian, but you're all Irish," he says, not meaning any disrespect toward my mom, but fond of the traits we share. I take a closer look at him. Behind the Buddy Holly glasses I notice bright blue eyes that crinkle just slightly when he smiles. He's black Irish: black hair (nearly shaved off), pale complexion, and those striking eyes. Mine are a lighter shade than his, and in the first-grade picture they are like glass orbs inside my little kid head. Lately I've been dying my brown-and-graying hair red and so I look even more the colleen.

More pictures yield more revelations. I show him a photo of me as a child with a few cousins and my Italian grandfather beneath the primitive grapevine gazebo he had fashioned out of scavenged materials for his family to eat under on warm summer Sundays. There's a black-and-white shot of Christmas-morning chaos, my mother looking radiantly sleepy as she helps my siblings with their presents. There's Easter Sunday with all five of us dressed in our best on the steps of our family home on Main Street with a globe in the porch window and a "The Kinsellas" sign on the front lawn. I tell him about my dad, who took most of the pictures: how he worked six days a week at his own lawn mower shop but rushed home to make my brother's Little League games. When they won, the whole team would pile in the back of my dad's El Camino and he'd treat everyone to ice cream at the Polar Cub.

Far from picture-perfect; nonetheless, we did have a good life.

Then I show him my favorite wedding picture: me sitting on the floor with my Cinderella dress spread out, my husband kneeling on it as we share a kiss. It has been seven years since we divorced, and try as I might, I am still devastated by it. I try to hide that from most people, but I'm probably not fooling the people who really know me, anyway.

After the picture show Rory tells me about his own relationships. For someone who has been in prison since he was nineteen, he's had his fair share. Even in here.

There was one woman who'd served time for drug dealing. She'd visit him often and even wanted to marry him, but he wouldn't let her because he felt it would be selfish. She died three years ago from hepatitis C, a drug-related illness. Years before, another woman had visited him wearing really short skirts (I have no idea how she pulled that off). He says the visiting staff used to be quite lax and that the configuration of tables outside once lent itself to more privacy. He smiles a crooked smile as he tells me how he and this woman managed to hide from the security cameras outside just long enough for him to bring her to sexual climax.

I try to remain composed.

"We would have gotten away with it, too, but she threw her head back," he tells me. "They came at us right away and took away my visits for six months. But it was worth it, just to see a woman's expression again at that moment."

Now I don't know these women, but I'm guessing they were very different from me. I've never shot up drugs. And I can't imagine getting it on in a prison yard.

Our summer day together passes quickly. At three o'clock (actually, five of, because the prison clock is fast) Buck Tooth gives the families back their passes and announces that visiting is over. We stand up and embrace. Rory squeezes so hard my spine pops. I feel sad about leaving him there in that horrible place and mumble "take care" into his neck.

Uncertain of procedure, I follow the other women as they shuffle out the door and pick up their IDs from the guard. Through the window women blow their men kisses. I wave to Rory and leave with the group.

One woman turns to me. "It's your first visit," she says, not asking but observing.

"Yeah, I guess it was obvious."

"You stood in the back of the room not knowing what to do just like I did the first time," she says with a smile.

I laugh, grateful for the friendly face. I don't notice anyone tapping on glass as we walk back up the path to the small cedar-shake visitor-processing building. The first mechanical gate opens and a handful of us step into the first pen. After it closes the second gate opens and we enter that pen. Huddled with these women I say to myself, now here's a sorority I don't want to join.

I fumble when the guard asks for my pass and ID. I am about to walk through the other side of the metal detector like the others have done when a guard tells me to step over to him. Clearly there is a choreography to all of this post-visit processing but I can't seem to get into step. The guard checks the stamp on my wrist under an ultraviolet light. Then I am free to go.

It is a seven-hour drive back to my home in the Bay Area. The first part of the trip is breathtaking—winding roads along rocky shores with the sun gleaming on whitecaps. Redwoods populate the mountains and often stand guard just inches off the road. I tell myself to drink it all in so that I can describe to Rory what absolute natural beauty lies just minutes from his gray walls.

Lost in thought, for the first two hours I do not even turn on the radio.

Rory couldn't help but fall in love with a woman like me. What does *that* mean, a woman like me? Alone in my head I do not have to be modest or politically correct. I may not be drop-dead gorgeous but I am attractive. Women know when they are and it is this silly game we play pretending we don't. (Rory had even said something to that effect earlier in the day.) I dress nicely, with a flare even. Cosmopolitan. I'm smart and a good conversationalist. I have led an interesting life. Okay, that's me. He's a convicted murderer. He rarely even sees women. But I care about him. I am kind to him. I encourage him. That is all genuine and more than he has received from anyone in years, I suppose. That's all this is, I tell myself, a lonely inmate's crush.

I think about the other women he's known: the drug dealer who died and the one with the short skirts and not much in the way of brains. I think of Amy the teenage siren who turned Rory on to shooting up. I stop myself in midjudgment of someone I have never met.

So many words exist for the sole purpose of categorizing people—especially women. Slut. Tramp. Whore. I search my brain for male words and think that "gigolo" or "cad" or "letch" just don't pack the same wallop as do so many derogatory expressions for women. What does it mean to be perceived as *that* kind of woman?

When I decided to visit Rory I promised my older brother that I would not fall in love with him and give my life away. "Can I get that in writing?" he said. We laughed. But now I am thinking about the women who do give their lives away to the incarcerated. One of the Menendez brothers married in prison. Women send Scott Peterson love letters on death row. But those are "celebrities." These guys are no one. What of these women then, the members of the sorority I've pledged not to pledge?

No one's life turns out exactly as expected—but what a drastic choice. My mind wanders back to the kind woman who spoke to me after the visit, and I realize I'd kept looking at her all day without really looking at her. Nameless, not faceless, I conjure up her image—plain, unassuming, even dowdy. My guess is she's ten years older than I am. I saw a simple gold band on her hand when the guard inspected her ID. She's white and looks a good five years older than her husband, a handsome, even dapper (not an easy feat in prison attire), African American man.

All I know of this woman is appearance and as I think about her this one horrible, assuming word keeps coming back to me.

Spinster.

Yes, I think, she would have been a spinster—alone without love if not for this. I imagine that Monday through Friday she's on her own with just twelve visiting hours on the weekend to be with her husband. Allowed only brief kisses and hand holding on top of a table in a sterile room or a concrete-and-barbed-wire-enclosed patio, is she not still a spinster on some level? But no life could possibly be summed up in a word. Besides, what makes me so different? My clothes? What of my Friday nights spent alone with rented movies and having that extra glass of white wine?

Spinster, know thyself.

The thought brings tears to my eyes. I fumble for a cassette to put in my ancient tape deck and come across one my ex-husband made for me when we were just dating. Cruising along the winding roads I try to steer my mind anywhere else. What a pathetic episode of *Sex and the City* the events of the day I just had would be.

And I just have to laugh. I think about that kind woman at the prison whom I'd been so quick to sum up in a word.

Next time I come to see Rory—in an instant I've committed to there being a next time—I decide I will talk with her and try to find out how she came to be living a visiting life.

CHAPTER 2

RUTH

Early in my prison-going experience I noticed that two things—both for their omnipresence and for their absence—hover above the visiting room: God and sex.

Just sitting in Ruth's car with her is enough to see which force guides her. "I'll be a sunbeam for Him!" says one of the stickers on the dashboard. "Jesus put a song in my heart!" says another. Ruth is the kind woman who spoke to me on my first visit to Pelican Bay. It took me a couple more visits and numerous little exchanges with her over the course of four months, but the last time I came to Crescent City I asked Ruth if she would share her story with me. She was eager to talk. She asked if I had read *The Prisoner's Wife* by Asha Bandele, a memoir written by a poet who married a man in prison. Ruth had lent me her copy. Apparently, it's made the rounds among the female visitors.

Now, it is a Saturday evening. This time it's on the record, and Ruth surprises me when she displays no signs of intimidation at the sight of my tape recorder and notebook. Perhaps I prejudged Ruth. As we drive to the Chinese restaurant I am thinking about what an unlikely pair of diners we make.

Ruth stands about five foot six but seems taller to me, perhaps because she has a tendency to wear long, flowing peasant-like jumper dresses or baggy sweaters over nondescript pants. She is turning fifty, but looks much younger. Worn long and straight with bangs, her hair is dyed her once-natural auburn, with gray roots showing just a touch at the temples. She wears gold wire-framed glasses. Her full face shines a pale white without the assistance of makeup. I bet she had freckles as a kid; her cheeks still have a chipmunk quality. Come to think of it, there is something childlike about both her appearance and her demeanor.

The Chinese restaurant is housed inside a converted family home. It is early for dinner—just after 5:00 p.m.—and only one other table is occupied, but we'd both spent the day at the prison and our stomachs are demanding some real food. I begin by asking about Bandele's book.

"I was surprised at how honest she was, especially about all the personal stuff with her husband," says Ruth. "I felt like I was reading her journal."

"When you loaned me the book, I asked you if you could relate to it, and you said, 'Yes and no,' " I say.

"Well, because of her attitude toward sex," Ruth explains, lowering her voice a little, out of modesty, I think, not self-consciousness. "She just went out there and figured, 'It's okay; I can do this.' " Even though Bandele and her husband enjoyed conjugal visits, she felt the need to seek out other male "friends." I suspect this is what Ruth is thinking about, but I do not want to lead her.

So she takes me there. "I talked with Burnard about that, and he just looked at me, like . . ." Her voice trails off, and she laughs softly. "I'd never do that, but some women have that attitude."

When she speaks about infidelity, there is no judgment in her voice. "You almost think, 'Why did you get involved with someone if you couldn't handle the fact of not being with that person in that way?' " Again, an observation, not a condemnation.

Ruth knows the isolation and loneliness of a prisoner's spouse. At best it is a Persephone-like experience where the free spouse straddles between two worlds, never quite belonging in either, as the Greek mythological daughter of Zeus and Demeter (goddess of the harvest) straddled between the earth and hell, the home of her captor-turned-husband, Hades. For the Greeks, the time Persephone spent in hell explained the seasons; Megan Comfort, a sociologist at the University of California in San Francisco, calls the separation-effect on women like Ruth "secondary prisonization." I am curious how it does or does not play out in Ruth's life. Yet, for the moment, I am amazed by how quickly we broached the topic of sex.

I had planned to approach sex gingerly, because when I first talked with Ruth at length she told me that she was molested as a child and had never really trusted men. I suspect that Ruth is still a virgin at fifty. Ironically, she works as a clerk in the local office of the state health department, a job in which she sometimes dispenses condoms without any real knowledge of how to use them.

"But I really liked the book," Ruth continues. "It made me realize things about her life and my life. What I didn't like is how her husband kept telling her it was going to get easier. That's why she kept coming back—she was waiting for that day when she felt comfortable coming in."

"Almost normal" is the phrase Bandele used to describe a life being married to an inmate.

"Did you and Burnard ever talk about that?" I ask.

"I don't know," Ruth says, searching her memory. "We never actually sat down and discussed how to handle it. I know my mom and dad at first were very cautious."

The story of Ruth and Burnard is a testament to the fact that life really can pivot on one little decision. For Ruth, it happened eight years ago, when she signed up for a Christmas program at her church in Southern California near where she grew up with her two big brothers and still lived with her parents.

An Angel Tree brought them together.

"The cards on the tree asked people to buy Christmas presents for children with fathers in prison," she explains. She picked Burnard's son because he wanted art supplies from the store where Ruth had bought her own supplies years ago, while she was earning a junior college degree in advertising art.

She had tried her hand at advertising but felt it was too cutthroat a world for her. At the time she picked the card off the Angel Tree she was doing order-entry work at a nondescript company not even worth mentioning and admits she didn't have much going on beyond that. "I didn't have a whole lot outside," she says, using an interesting choice of words, considering where her husband lives.

She bought the art supplies, and her mother added a few extra trinkets to the package. Her father drove her over to deliver the presents to the boy. Though wary about their daughter getting involved on any level with a person in prison, her parents also believed in charity.

Through the Angel Tree program Ruth was given the option of writing to the inmate. "I really felt that I was supposed to do that. But what do you say?" She sent a Christmas card and was surprised when Burnard wrote back.

The waitress brings us our food. Ruth fumbles with her

chopsticks and says she is not very good with them but always gives them a try.

"In his first letter he didn't seem to want to stop writing. He kept saying, 'I should let you go,' " she says, laughing a little. "And then he didn't know if I was married. He said to say 'Hi to your husband.' He was protecting himself."

More likely, I'm thinking, he was fishing for information.

When I first started writing to Rory, a former defense attorney friend of mine told me to be very careful with disclosing personal information. "They can seem so nice, I know," she said. "But they are master manipulators."

Manipulated or not, here sits bright-eyed Ruth giggling and blushing like a schoolgirl as she talks about the beginning of her relationship with her husband. They have been married over three years now, having known each other for four before. "I think it was by the fourth letter that he was writing, 'Can't we be more than friends,' " Ruth remembers. "He was ready to jump really fast and I wasn't. I quoted something about that which grows slowly takes longer but is very sturdy."

She filled her early letters to Burnard with her Christianity: passages from scripture and quotes from other religious material she read. Raised a Catholic, Ruth admits she never felt comfortable with the Church. She says she didn't even want to be alive. "When I was younger I wrote a letter to God and told him, 'If you don't do something, I'm going to do something,' because I wasn't happy with my life," she says in her flat, unanimated way of speaking about even the most dramatic things. "I didn't really talk to anyone when I was young, and I think that was a problem. I kept everything in. I wanted to call one of those hotlines." Instead she wrote to God and befriended a woman who would lead her to be born again, not that Ruth was open to that at first.

"If she had asked me right away to accept Jesus as my Lord and savior, I would have laughed. Yeah, right," Ruth recalls. Ultimately the friend's message resonated with Ruth, who became a born-again Christian at twenty-three.

In the "honeymoon" phase of her new faith, she made tracts and left them at restaurants and other public places. "Tracks?" I ask, mispronouncing the word. Little notes talking to Jesus that invite others to join the conversation, she explains. I'm picturing those notes selling guitar lessons or babysitting services posted outside of supermarkets. She got a few calls from the tracts, and even went out with a couple of men who responded, but nothing romantic materialized.

"Burnard says that God was protecting me because I was so innocent," she says, deflecting to her husband. "I'd go out with these guys and I didn't even know them. It could be a scary thing." One time she even left a note on a stranger's car. "I can't believe I did that." She remembers that they met at Denny's, then went back to his place and read from Genesis. "I would see him after that but nothing happened," she says. Later, the young man told her he had been depressed and even suicidal. "Maybe, through me, God showed him that somebody who didn't even know him cared."

For clarity I have to ask, "So, you've never actually physically been with a man?" She surprises me with an answer that shows neither hesitation nor timidity, but does betray a tinge of defiance. "Almost was."

It was right after graduating from junior college, a few years before her Christian conversion. "Actually, I was molested as a child," she says, repeating herself. "That made me more willing to just do it, just to say I did it."

Again she defers to her husband: "Burnard says that God

protected me, because once a guy starts he doesn't stop. So I'm really grateful it didn't happen." What did happen is that she visited a friend and was left alone in the apartment when the telephone repairman arrived. "You know how you hear stories about the telephone repairman?" she says nonchalantly, quietly laughing again, as seems her way of dealing with touchy or complicated subjects. They got to talking and she told him she was nineteen and had just graduated from junior college. He had offered to give her a graduation kiss. "I remember it was a little bit more than a kiss and it was accelerating and part of me just wanted to do it," she says. "But I'm glad I didn't."

She hasn't thought about it in years. "If I told people at work they'd be so shocked because they think I am this totally quiet person. Even when I tell Burnard, he's kind of shocked." Heck, I'm thinking, I'm kind of shocked, though I am not sure why I should be. I'm glad she is laughing and enjoying the memories unfettered by any guilt or self-consciousness. Perhaps there should be a little egg foo yong on my face for assuming this seemingly simple woman, terribly wounded as a child, had had no amorous experience.

By this time the fortune cookies have arrived. I give Ruth first shot at the future. "You're ambitious and may make a name for yourself," she reads. "That's not me at all. Ambitious!"

Ruth never expected to have a life on her own much less a life with a partner, which, I imagine, intensifies her appreciation for what she now has for herself and with Burnard. I watch Ruth fiddle with the fortune cookie and comment about her rings—a simple gold wedding band on one hand and a more ornamental though still modest ring on her right index finger. As she stretches out her hands I am struck by their beauty—elongated, like those of a Madonna in a Mannerist painting. She tells me that her parents gave her the other ring when she was twenty-six, after her brother got engaged. "They said, 'You need a nice ring,' " she explains. I can only imagine how hurt my unmarried older sister would have been if my parents had given her a ring after I got engaged at twenty-six. But Ruth simply accepted the gift, never giving thought to the slight it might imply. Years after the dawn of feminism, we still have a long way to go before women are truly liberated from the antiquated notion that no man means no life.

Ruth simply never felt such notions applied to her.

While Ruth visits her husband every weekend, I visit Rory less frequently and a couple of months pass before I see her again. This time I remind Ruth that I'd like to see her wedding pictures, and she invites me over to her place that evening.

The minute Ruth entered her two-bedroom apartment in Crescent City, she says, she felt right at home, which was odd because she hadn't planned to live here. She came up on an extended vacation to help another woman she met through the prison get settled. Then Ruth got laid off and decided to stay a little longer. When Ruth stumbled onto a job in Crescent City and her friend decided she didn't want to live there anymore, Ruth felt as if all signs were telling her to take the apartment for herself. That was five years ago. "My parents still think I planned it, but I told them they could read my journals," she says. Ruth still writes to God but now they are daily letters kept in a notebook as a chronicle of her life and not a threat against it.

Ruth's apartment building occupies a block of what passes for a downtown here—a Safeway, a few restaurants, plenty of fast-food joints and economy motels, a bowling alley, and a couple of bars. The museum, ironically, is housed in the old jail. In 1964 a tsunami crushed Crescent City (named for the shape of its bay), demolishing most of its downtown. At 3:36 a.m. on March 28, the largest earthquake ever recorded in North America—measuring 9.2 on the Richter scale—struck off the northern shore of Alaska's Prince William Sound. The shock reverberated through the ocean and a few hours later the first two swells hit Crescent City. At 7:08 a.m. the sheriff evacuated downtown, and soon after the ocean completely receded out of the rather large bay, leaving boats anchored offshore abandoned in the mud. Two more waves rushed through the emptied bay and broke on the little city, knocking buildings off their foundations. Only a few old Victorian-style homes remained.

Ruth's garden-style apartment sits in the rebuilt section of town, now known as Tsunami Landing. The local economy depends largely on fishing and on Pelican Bay State Prison, which opened in 1989. A few blocks from the Pacific, Ruth's apartment is about five miles from the prison where her husband has lived for more than a decade. He is serving life without parole, but I am not yet sure of the details surrounding his incarceration beyond the charge being drug-related and that Ruth believes he is innocent.

"I try to tell Burnard that this is my sanctuary," says Ruth as she shows me around. "It's not that big, but can you imagine if the guys were here? It would seem like a palace." Ruth always calls the inmates "the guys."

The pale green walls are covered with all sorts of pictures that lean on the cute side, framed scriptures, and other affirmations. Many of the wall decorations are cards and pictures from Burnard. A fake miniature redwood stands in the living room's bay window, festooned with birds on its branches and myriad

stuffed critters below. I'd describe the decor as somewhere between Holly Hobbie and Laura Ashley. It suits Ruth.

In the master bedroom, which Ruth uses as an office, prefer-
ring the smaller room for her twin bed, hangs a portrait of the
couple that Burnard "commissioned" from another inmate.

"It's amazing what they can do," I say. Prohibited from having paints and canvases, artistically inclined inmates fashion a
palette from ground-up colored pencils mixed with water, create a brush with their own hair, and paint on old bedsheets.
Voilà: a "masterpiece" created with something akin to pastels or
watercolors. Since there is so little the inmates can give their
friends and families even the smallest offering takes on greater
significance.

Like Ruth's necklace.

Ruth wears two pendants on a single metal chain: a cross and
a heart that Burnard crafted from discarded optical lenses he ac-
quired while he was working in the prison's eyeglass clinic. He
fused together tints to make the charms purple, the couple's favorite color. "I don't think they have that Arts in Corrections
Program anymore, which is sad because they need that outlet,"
says Ruth, starting off on a tangent. "Burnard took a few classes
in creative writing. And they even had a movie night and they
showed silent movies. What was neat was that after the movie—
since it was at night—when they walked out they could see the
stars. They don't get to see the stars."

Rory had once told me that what he missed most about the
outside world was the moon.

In the living room, Ruth and I sit together on the couch with
a "friends are the best thing in life" pillow between us. A collection of stuffed "friends" sits across the back of the sofa. Ruth
makes some comment about dust as she pats the pillow. I joke

that I would not be so quick to pat something in my own apartment while entertaining. Spending every weekend at the prison leaves Ruth with little time for housekeeping, but the place is clean and cozy.

"This is the first picture he sent," she says, opening an attractive but not fancy dime-store variety photo album. "He told me I should get rid of it because he looks mean." A less gray, leaner Burnard stares at the camera. His skin is dark and smooth; his features chiseled. He is handsome but does look mean, or, at the very least, guarded and hard. "I don't think it looks like him at all," says Ruth.

"He has such a nice smile," I offer, thinking of the Burnard I have glanced at across the visiting room. The guards try to prohibit cross-visiting—for example, chatting with an inmate you are not approved to visit—so I haven't said more than hello to Ruth's husband. But I have sized him up a bit. Although I've never seen him in anything except his prison denim, he walks with the gait of a man who'd be a sharp dresser if given the chance. He is a little shorter than Ruth and thirteen years her junior. If he didn't have some gray hair, he'd look much younger.

"See, you don't smile in prison," Ruth lightly mocks. "That was before I met him."

She turns the page and Burnard appears with another inmate whom Ruth calls his common-law brother-in-law. Burnard has been married twice before and has children with an ex-wife and another woman he lived with. "He's really tall," says Ruth about the other man. "It's strange, because he's actually the guy who killed the guy who Burnard allegedly told him to kill."

This is the first I learn that Burnard is serving life for murder or a murder-related charge. While friends, family, and strangers will easily ask about someone's crime and/or guilt or innocence, it is a subject handled delicately among the visitor population. History seems a safer place to start.

Ruth says that Burnard was born in the South and that his father had very little to do with him. She suspects that his father didn't know how to spell Bernard, thus the unusual spelling of her husband's name. His mother moved to Southern California with her nine children, most of them her own, though she also took in others. She died when Burnard was twelve. The children did whatever they could to survive and miraculously managed to stay out of the foster care system. Burnard stole whatever he could and landed in the California Youth Authority. He graduated to drug dealing and got caught again. He had been in and out of the prison system ever since. Once, back on the street, he even wore a wire as a police informant. Then he got set up for the murder for which Ruth provides no details. This is what he told Ruth, and she believes him. I'm not so sure I do.

Looking at the photo with his brother-in-law, she says, "I asked him, 'Why didn't he just say you didn't do it?' " Her voice softens and weakens a little. "Well, I don't know what that's all about. You never know, right?" She sounds resigned to not having all the pieces of the puzzle in place.

After she moved to Crescent City her parents came to meet Burnard. The prison was in lockdown at the time, which included even the inmates not involved in the incident that caused it. Contact visits were restricted. "He was behind glass," says Ruth. "And he said it was a good thing because then my parents couldn't pound him." Far from pounding him, Ruth's parents embraced him. They, too, get their strength from their Christianity. Her parents are even paying for Burnard's legal fees, and his case has just made it to the federal appellate court. "That really surprised me," says Ruth. "I think they feel sorry for me."

Ruth turns the page and her face brightens as she chuckles at the image of herself. "That's your Ma and Pa Kettle picture," I say, remembering how she had once told me that in the first picture she took with Burnard they looked like that farmer couple depicted in the painting *American Gothic* by Grant Wood. Neither one smiles. They stand shoulder to shoulder but do not touch. Their expressions are identical, blank, startled, like the proverbial deer caught in headlights. "When I came in with that dress, the officer said, 'Well, we won't have to worry about this one,' and I didn't know what he meant," says Ruth. She is wearing one of the smock dresses that her mother made. If some women have "trouble" written all over them, Ruth has just the opposite word—whatever that is. "I guess he figured anyone who dresses like that isn't going to do anything," she adds.

Her maiden visit occurred on Labor Day weekend in 1997. "I was shocked that my mother didn't say anything when I said I was going to visit," she says. "I guess she figured I was old enough to do what I wanted."

"Were you nervous?" I ask.

Fate, or as Ruth would prefer to see it, God, didn't give her the chance to be nervous for herself. In Crescent City's tiny coastal airport she met two women who spoke very little English but who Ruth learned were also going to Pelican Bay for the first time. "They were praying and I was praying, so we hooked up," she says. "It's funny; here I was praying I can help somebody when I didn't even know what I'm doing."

They couldn't find the prison at first. It's easy to miss. Only a stoplight out of nowhere on a county road marks the entrance. There is no sign until you turn into the facility. Cars proceed at 20 mph around the 275 acres of fenced-in buildings and yards that house approximately 3,300 inmates in separate facilities for

Level I (the lowest security), Level IV (the highest for general population inmates), Psych Ward, and supermax for snitches and offenders who committed crimes while in prison. It is a formidable place for any first-time visitor.

Little has changed in its appearance in seven years, but Ruth says that the guards at Pelican Bay were not as helpful back then as they are now. "A lot of the women came and helped," she adds. "They were asking me all these questions. 'How'd you meet him? Are you going to kiss him?' " What she remembers most about those first three days together is how easily the conversation flowed. "I could talk to guys but they never seemed to communicate back. With Burnard, when we met, we just talked. I wish I could remember all that we said, but we just talked the whole time."

They held hands while they prayed together, but Burnard took his hand back. "He told me later that he wanted to hold my hand, but he knew about my past and he didn't want to be too aggressive," she says. Is he manipulating her, I wonder, but do not interrupt. "Even the first time we held hands, I felt comfortable. It felt right." Simpatico from the start, but Burnard still caught Ruth off guard with his final good-bye.

More than twenty years had passed since Ruth experienced a French kiss. So, at forty-two, Ruth did what pretty much every middle-school kid does when playing spin the bottle. "I didn't know what to do, but I thought if I didn't respond he's going to think something's wrong," she says. "So I responded. That one shocked me."

By the time she returned for her second visit, this time on New Year's weekend, something had clearly shifted for both of them. It's obvious in the pictures. This time Burnard's arm is around Ruth's shoulder, and they both smile. Ruth beams in a way all women beam when they are with the man who tells them they are beautiful. That's when she told her mother that she left her heart in Crescent City. "It's funny looking at some of the old pictures. I first came here never realizing that I would live here," she says. Let alone that she'd become a prison wife. "It's almost like God had to pry me out of that house."

Now her face lights up whenever she says her husband's name.

"No one ever told me I was beautiful before," she says. "He tells me, 'Can't you just look in the mirror and see it?' After all the years of people saying you're not . . ." She trails off. "He gets mad at me."

I say how it's nice to be told you are beautiful.

"Yeah, it is, but *sexy?*" she says, with another laugh. "It's so funny; we were talking about [the movie] *Freaky Friday.* He says that 'if I were in you, I'd just be naked all the time.' I'm like, what?" She laughs that little laugh again, clearly liking his attention.

"Do you want him sexually?" I ask.

"Well," she pauses. "Yeah," she answers in a singsong voice that stretches the word out to three syllables. "I tell him that if I can't be with you then I won't be with anybody. And that made him feel good. I feel very comfortable with him and I've never felt that."

People might judge Ruth, but she doesn't seem to care. Certainly I judged her as a would-be spinster. Oh, I was kinder about my judgment than it sounds, even going on to wonder if perhaps no one had ever told this woman she was pretty. Turns out I was right. But there's so much more to the paradox that is Ruth—or at least the part of her she let me see.

She's a survivor of childhood molestation, a born-again

Christian, a virgin at fifty who works for the California health department and sometimes distributes condoms. She has never physically been with any man and yet lives for her husband. Ruth rarely takes a weekend off from visiting.

I imagine that Ruth's innocence shepherds her from the desire and frustration a sexually active woman might feel in her situation. I remember when I was in college and felt like the only virgin alive and wondered even more if I was a freak because I didn't seemed obsessed with sex like everybody else. My roommate—also Catholic, also a virgin—came up with the "Chocolate Cake Theory of Sex": basically, if you've never eaten chocolate cake and didn't know how great chocolate cake was, then you couldn't miss it or even know how much you wanted to try it. The same rationale, we speculated, might apply to sex. We were naive college students but that didn't make us sexless. Ruth's sexuality might be naive, but it is her sexuality.

When she dreams of Burnard, she dreams of taking a walk together on the beach or making dinner in her kitchen. "I've had weird dreams where he's out, or he's out but he has some sort of curfew and he has to go back," as if even in her subconscious the bars cannot fully dissolve.

"I'm sure Burnard dreams of family visits," I say, using the polite term for conjugal visits. Whether Ruth thinks about it or not, bottom line, it's what outsiders wonder about and what insiders learn about early on. In 1996 California governor Pete Wilson rescinded conjugal visitation rights for lifers, sex offenders, and inmates with a history of domestic abuse. Regardless of their political leanings, the inmates saw hope in the election of Arnold Schwarzenegger because, as Rory told me, "The last time we had an actor governor [Ronald Reagan], he gave us those visits." And so they hope. There is a case currently pending in California about restoring family visits. I am not sure if Ruth is hoping that such privileges will be restored. She quickly answers my question, but I do not think it is a topic she wishes to explore.

"Oh, he would love to be . . ." she starts to say. "Someone said to me that guys don't just think about sex they think about fishing, too. I said, 'Well, my husband doesn't like to fish.' " And that pretty much is the end of that line of thought.

I want to look at her wedding pictures, anyway.

While her family grew to accept Burnard and Ruth's special circumstances, not everyone in Ruth's life was so kind. Two of her close friends are completely against it. One, the woman who was the instrument to her Christianity, went so far as to tell Ruth that she had had a vision and that God was against their union. "You never know how people are going to react," Ruth says. "Burnard says that once someone knows you have someone in prison they think you are desperate."

After her wedding, she visited with her family in Southern California and put the wedding album together there. She missed out on the traditional bridal shower, but her friends— even the one who had the vision—and family gathered to see her photographs. Her parents and two friends had made the trip up to Crescent City and witnessed the wedding on June 15, 2001. Ruth wore a white smock dress with purple flowers on it and a white turtleneck that she'd found on sale at Wal-Mart. Burnard was in his prison blues, but he wore his best pants and had even managed to crease them. This was no easy accomplishment: irons are prohibited in prison, of course. So the inmates fill a plastic bottle with water from their toilet that they had heated with a stinger, a contraption that conducts an electric charge from the outlet and brings it into the toilet. They then rub the heated water bottle across their pants.

"I told him that that dress was fine because it was one of the first dresses I wore here. We both like purple and it had flowers on it and we couldn't have flowers." Ruth has seen several weddings take place in that visiting room. "There was a girl who actually wore a wedding dress," she says. "To me, that's a bit much in that setting. Then some don't get dressed up at all."

The first picture in the album is their wedding portrait, which they actually staged the next day because in all the excitement they forgot to snap the classic bride-and-groom pose. On the facing page is an announcement her parents made for the occasion: "Mr. and Mrs. [her parents' name] wish a lifetime of happiness to Ruth and Burnard [their full names] as they become one in the sight of God." Then the date and the location for the ceremony: "The Patio at Pelican Bay."

"How may pictures do they let you take?" I ask.

"As many as you want." It depends on how many ducats the inmate managed to stash away for the occasion. Photo ducats cost $2 apiece; one ducat gets you one Polaroid. Burnard and Ruth took eleven wedding pictures. Inmates often earn less than 30 cents an hour, so getting together $22 took some doing. But Burnard put in as much time as he could at his eyeglass lab job and saved up. Ruth fattened the album out with notes, scriptures, and tokens to remember the day. They were not allowed to write their own vows, but Ruth appreciates how the chaplain made it special and appropriate for their unique union. The vows are traditional for the most part, but also include these passages:

Even though there are many other people in the various buildings around us right now, here together, you stand free and apart from all other people in this world because right now you stand within the circle of your love for one another and that is exactly where you should be.

Now in the coming weeks and months ahead you may be physically separated from each other but this love you have and the commitments you are about to make should give you the strength and courage to face whatever problems you may come up with until that special day comes when you are united forever.

So from this day forward you must come closer together than ever before. You must love one another in sickness and in health, for better or for worse; but at the same time your love should also give you the strength to stand apart, to seek out your own unique destinies and to make your own special contributions to the world, which is always part of us.

The vows end with the phrase, "You may kiss your lovely bride."

"So you got an extra kiss," I say.

"And we got the picture," she answers. I hadn't thought how that would be the only occasion when the couple would be allowed to photograph themselves kissing. "Actually, the officer took some of these pictures."

There's a wide shot of the wedding in progress as Burnard says his vows and then a close-up of their entwined hands wearing their wedding bands. There's even a funny one of them feeding each other wedding cake, or rather slices of banana cake from the vending machine.

"You do what you can," says Ruth.

There are photos from the night before with Ruth and her mom, who had just put the bride-to-be's hair in rollers. Among the keepsakes in the album is the first card addressed to them as husband and wife. Ruth's aunt, a nun, had sent it. The card reads: "Love knows no limits to its endurance, no end to its trust, no fading of its heart. Love never fails. (1 Corinthians 13:7–8)." Her mother cut up some of the photos, placing the bridal party in a more festive setting. So here's a shot of Burnard and Ruth placing rings on each other's fingers under a garden trellis. No one is going to be fooled by this ruse, but there's not a whole lot you can do to dress up a wedding performed against drab, gray walls.

Ruth closes the album and pats the cover. "I was surprised when a woman at work said she wanted to get me a present," she says about the album. She was surprised, too, when her parents put her wedding pictures alongside those from her brothers' weddings. "They made it seem real."

I find myself telling Ruth how I saw two of my women friends, partners of seventeen years, get married in San Francisco City Hall and featured on a segment of *The NewsHour with Jim Lehrer.* "I'm not sure how you feel about that," I say, trying not to offend this Christian woman in her own home by talking about same-sex marriage. "But I bought them a present because I wanted to honor their marriage knowing that others would not."

"Well, I don't agree with that, but who am I to tell people what to do?" she says, without any resentment. "Those things are hard." She goes on to tell me about a gay man in her office and how in not-very-cosmopolitan Crescent City he cannot act as freely as he could in a place like San Francisco. "That's gotta be hard," she repeats. "It's kind of like even in my situation, not telling people what's going on." Once again, Ruth surprises me. But as with any multifaceted idea that has come up in our conversations, Ruth—without displaying any undue discomfort— quickly scoots right along and away from it.

She prefers to discuss how some people can be harsh when she tells them about Burnard. "Some of them go, 'Can I ask what he did?' A lot of people ask me when he is going to get out," she explains. "When I say, 'Maybe never,' then you get this look like 'Why on earth?' "

Why, then?

"Burnard says an angel brought us together," says Ruth. "When I met him he wasn't really close to God. He was mad at God and saying, 'How dare you put me in this prison.' Excuse me? You made the decisions that landed you there." Ruth may not know all the particulars of Burnard's past, but she knows enough not to give him a pass on his drug-dealing former life that may or may not include murder. She acknowledges that prison might have saved him. "Some people say prison's a good thing because they get backed into a corner and they have to reevaluate their life. And Burnard says that then he would never have met me."

Ruth belongs to that "everything happens for a reason" school. And, for her, that reason is God's to understand. Even when it comes to sex, apparently. When I ask Ruth if some part of her is afraid that the law will return family visits for lifers or that Burnard will get out, she says, "I just pray that God prepares us for the answer." I note the use of the word "us."

A psychologist might look at Ruth and surmise that for a woman who was sexually traumatized as a child, a marriage to a man serving life without parole is simply safe. For her, it is simply her marriage. Strong in her faith, Ruth soldiers along on a path she never expected to tread. It's a path that led to prison, true, but also to love. Besides, she gets to feel beautiful. Even if Ruth and Burnard are destined to live life apart, they are not living life alone.

CHAPTER 3

THE GETAWAY GIRL

I am not sure whom I surprised more with my second visit to prison, Rory or me. It happened sooner than I had expected and turned out to be an escape mission.

My escape, not his, of course.

As mad as I have been with God over the years, I have to admit that He manages to throw the right person into my path just when I need him or her most. The summer I met Rory I tried fiercely not to see him as that person.

At the time I told myself I was just filling an empty August weekend with a road trip. In reality I was in the middle of some sort of breakdown all summer but was too strong or too stubborn, or both, to let myself break. Why not make the seven-hour drive up to Crescent City and get my mind off things? It's not like Rory wouldn't be there; one good thing about visiting someone in prison, you've got a captive audience.

Still, the idea that Rory finds me a little too captivating concerned me. After our first visit he sent a glowing letter about an incident with an inmate who wanted Rory to hook him up with whatever "stuff" had been making him feel so good lately. "Dude, she's one of a kind and I ain't sharin'," Rory replied. After making some small talk the guy quickly sulked away because, as Rory wrote, "The only thing worse than being around a drunk when you are sober is being around someone who's happy-giddy-in-love when you're lonely."

In love? That can't be good. And loneliness, I know all too well. Putting the two together can be lethal even under the most normal of circumstances; both of us were in jeopardy. So the next time he called collect I stressed how our relationship could only be of a platonic nature. He said he understood, but I'm not so sure I believed him.

About a week later a fat envelope with that pencil printing I recognized so well showed up in my mailbox. In his letter, Rory tried to address both of our fears: mine, that he loves me inappropriately, and his, that he might ruin the most precious friendship of his life with his archaic notions of romance. From the very beginning our correspondence danced around the age-old questions of love. In the new novel Rory was working on, titled *No Hero,* he used characters he created to work out his own issues. "It's mostly about addiction," Rory wrote about the book-in-progress. "My addiction to love, or rather, the ideal of love, and about people's absurd fears being an excuse, and their desire to <u>be</u> heroes, or their <u>need</u> for a belief in one whether it be God or man."

He admitted that he was writing the latest letter under the influence of Pelican Bay's home brew ("pruno," they call it, a sort of wine made from anything they can ferment), and I interpreted the letter as an inmate's version of drunk dialing. He said I am the inspiration for *No Hero*'s direction. "Especially the close analyzation (shit, is that even a word?) you spark in me of my own feelings and emotions, my brain-induced chemical addiction to love and the tragic end it would have, always has for me." Yeah, I knew he was playing with my sympathies here, but I also accepted it when he said he would swallow his feelings and just be the best friend I could ever want.

On some level I envied Rory. He didn't have to work out the complexities of life while juggling all of the pressures of the real world; he could live in a fictional world to explore them. Of course such "freedom" came at an unbearable price—one I could not endure, I know. I also admired him for attempting to grow emotionally from such a terribly oppressive place. But what did he really have to lose by tossing his heart over the wall to me? Don't get me wrong; his letters and affection provided a real emotional support I treasured and so desperately wanted. But I couldn't live in letters. I wanted a partner in life again—or at least a boyfriend. So I was relieved as I read on in his twelve-page drunken ramblings that he understood what I could and could not be for him.

"I'm not so stupid as to think for one second that a smart, beautiful, 'Cosmo' girl like yourself would fall in love with a convict doing life-without-parole in prison," he wrote. "Well, maybe for a second." (Then he drew a smiley face.) He said it's his trip and that he can deal with it. "But I swear, if you're lonely at sixty you are totally gonna be mine." Okay, I guess a girl needs a plan B, I thought. Besides, I needed all the laughter I could find.

The pieces of my life were shifting like shards of glass in a kaleidoscope. I tried to decipher the crazy configurations piece by piece. First, work. Being an agent wasn't working out so well. I had a handful of clients and as much as I liked working with them on their projects and proposals, I couldn't sell anything. So I decided to go back to my job at *Publishers Weekly,* the book trade magazine I had worked at for ten years. The only problem with that was, like so many magazines facing declining ad sales,

Publishers Weekly was in severe cost-cutting mode when I approached my editor about coming back to work. So, even though she was a huge fan of my work, she could only offer me a meager stipend that was less than half of what I had been making before. Upside: the new/old job would take only two days a week. I weighed my options and took it with the intention of using the extra time to work on my own writing.

The best part about being a correspondent covering the publishing business is that it comes with a ready-made social scene. In just two years' time living in California working as a journalist then agent then journalist again, I had successfully transitioned my New York publishing life for a West Coast version—even if I wasn't making much of a living at it. I went on fancy lunches with publishers, attended author readings at bookstores, and went to cocktail parties at art galleries. When *San Francisco Magazine* ran an article about the Bay Area book scene it named me as "a person who knows everybody in the biz."

But what good is being "connected" when your personal life feels like one giant disconnection? Each click of the kaleidoscope revealed an emptiness where the colorful shards of my dreams should have been. I tried to fill it with work.

When people ask me why I decided to move from New York to California at the age of thirty-seven and seemingly at the top of my career, I either lie or half-lie. Why would I leave a job with the column inches that enabled me to help make or break news about books, a lifelong passion? The lie I tell is that *Publishers Weekly* sent me to California. The truth is, I marched into my editor's office one day, burned out, and announced that I had to move somewhere. She suggested California, where they needed a new correspondent. The half-lie I tell is that like so many Americans before me, I moved West to reinvent myself.

The real truth, the one I know when I lie awake at night trying to dream of a new future, is that I grew tired of swallowing myself up. When Rory wrote to me about swallowing his feelings, I knew exactly what he meant.

As much as I love my family, I found it hard to be around them. Divorced, devastated, and childless (the clincher): it became unbearable for me to be at family gatherings with everybody else's kids. Oh, I am not proud of myself. It's not like anyone in the family ever made me feel bad about being divorced; in fact, they hardly talked to me about it at all. Really, what's to say? "Sorry, Bridge." And so I'd swallow myself—or at least the bitterness I felt—in order to be as much in the present and with my family as I could.

The funny thing is (and by funny I mean sad), I think I was once one of the happiest people in the family.

There's nothing like being surrounded by a big family when you are getting married. That is certainly how I felt back in 1990 when Alexei, the first boyfriend I really ever had, asked me to marry him. No one was surprised; we'd been dating for three years and they had gotten to know and love him at family gatherings. I was twenty-six; he was twenty-three. My Italian uncles joked about how bringing Alexei's lean six-foot-four Russian frame into the family gene pool might get us some height and how his strawberry blond hair might bring some more natural red back into the family. (My Italian grandfather, gone for a few years by then, had had red hair and blue eyes.)

We took only six months to plan the wedding: 120 guests, black tie optional, at a grand old hotel on the New Jersey shore.

When some people marry it can take them away from their families; my marriage brought me even closer to mine.

Young love energizes a family. Everyone got involved. My parents paid for the reception. Alexei and I provided incidentals—my wedding dress, the flowers, the booze. My brothers furnished the band: a five-piece ensemble that could play everything from rock and swing to the tango. My youngest cousin played the oboe in the church. I could practically hear my uncle Jack's laughing Irish eyes over the phone when he called nightly for the "countdown" leading up to the big day. My mom and my sisters gave me an elaborate shower—and I can still remember each and every gift and who gave it to us. I even enjoyed writing the thank-you notes, because, unlike what I have heard about other big weddings that are really more about the parents than the kids, ours really was about us. Most of the guests had watched me grow up. Some of Alexei's family came down from Maine and, for the occasion at least, put aside their differences with their New Jersey relatives after decades of a family rift.

I knew we were lucky.

In the months leading up to the big day I lived with my parents in the two-bedroom condo on the beach they rented after selling the family home. On workdays I'd mount a bus for New York before sunrise and return long after sunset, but I never minded it. Alexei visited often, and the four of us planned the wedding together. My mother found the centerpieces on sale at Fortunoff. On a shoe-shopping excursion I said to my mom, "They always say that you marry your father, but Daddy and Alexei are nothing alike." Alexei the artist and my dad the mechanic, who at the height of his career owned his own lawn mower shop. "I don't know," my mother said, "Alexei and your father have one thing in common: they are both kind men."

While we were out shoe shopping, my dad drove Alexei around to hotels where we might spend our wedding night.

"Wasn't that weird?" I asked Alexei later.

"Dad didn't make it weird," he said, trying on the familial moniker for my father that he would never really find comfortable. "Besides, it's not like we set out to look at hotel rooms, we were just driving around on other errands and your dad said, 'Hey, why don't we just take a look?' " I wondered if they'd had some man-to-man talk.

Even though Alexei was an art student and worked at a record store, my parents never questioned his ability to earn a living; besides, they knew we'd work together as a team. "I lost my job a few weeks before my wedding," my father told us one night after dinner. For better or worse, my parents have always been risk takers; for the most part it worked out. My dad heard about a job when they called in from their honeymoon in Washington, D.C., but instead of running back home he decided they should take a few extra days in New York to celebrate. He still got the job.

For our big day we decided on black-and-white photography, and when we looked at my parents' wedding album together, Alexei won my mother over for life when he told her she looked like a young Liz Taylor. She had the short black coiffed hair and 1950s style down, but, while curvy, my mom couldn't have been more than ninety-eight pounds. "A full-figured size two," I teased her. My dad looked debonair in his tux tails with his hair combed up in a slick black pompadour. "He got better looking as he got older," my mom said. In his sixties my dad has thick white hair, crystal eyes, and a ruddy complexion. I like to say that I inherited my father's face and my mom's figure, although in a slightly larger package.

As Alexei and I planned our wedding we'd eagerly listen to stories about my parents' ceremony and their newlywed days. My dad called his wedding simply "the best party he ever attended." Their wedding had its drama, too: an ice storm the night before almost prevented it from happening. We all agreed that their best wedding picture shows my mom sitting on the dance floor with her white dress spread around her like a silk-satin snowdrift, my father kneeling on it as they share a kiss.

I think we all fell in love with the idea of romance—theirs and ours. And my favorite prenuptial memory is of the four of us moving the living room furniture so we could practice old-fashioned couples dancing. My mom refused to tell us how tall she was anymore after losing a few inches to age, but standing barely five feet she looked ridiculous dancing with Alexei. The two of them had their own little romance; Alexei often bought my mom chocolates that she'd squirrel away.

In the months leading up to the wedding, our family and friends made us feel like we were the center of the universe. Even a downpour on the morning of the wedding didn't dampen our spirits. After the ceremony, my best friend's mother commented that she'd never seen a father of the bride walk down the aisle waving to people as if he were the mayor, saying, "Hey, how ya doin?" "Great to see ya." I wore a blusher over my face to avoid making eye contact with anyone who might make me cry.

The most important moments in life somehow don't feel like they are happening. Everything seemed like a dream that day—the rustic seaside church, the sound of the wedding march. The only thing that snapped me back into my own body was when I took Alexei's hand at the altar. I really believe that this was the moment we were married. I remember thinking that no matter what happened ahead, so long as we held each other's hands, all would be fine. We may have fallen in love with romance, but the reality of my parents' long union with its ups and downs served as a good example of the work involved in the commitment we'd just made.

When we posed for a picture with me sitting on the dance floor, my white dress a silk-satin snowdrift, and Alexei kneeling in for a kiss, it seemed a fitting tribute.

So we began our life. Alexei managed the record store where we met and once worked together. He finished his undergraduate work in fine arts. I had my magazine job in the city and finished up my undergrad work in economics and English at night. We bought our own little house on Main Street in one of those quaint bedroom communities along the train route to New York. We decorated it ourselves with wedding mementos and Alexei's artwork. Much of our furniture came from weekend antiquing trips to Lambertville along the Delaware River. We had a favorite shop there that was owned by a slightly older couple who took a fancy to us, the newlyweds. The wife was an artist like Alexei and they'd talk art while the husband, an adorable Brit, took to teasing me like a big brother. I thought I was pretty sly with my attraction for the guy, but then one time, as we were getting out of the car in front of the shop, Alexei teased, "I wonder if *Malcolm* is going to be there?" sort of singing the name. I blushed. "Oh, please, Bridget, like I can't tell when you are attracted to someone?" he said, with no tone of jealousy in his voice. Trust was never a question between us. In fact, the highest compliment Alexei ever gave me—and he said it only a handful of times—reflected the nonjealous nature of our bond. "I love how other men look at you." I was wearing a classic black evening dress I had borrowed from my sister Claire when he whispered it to me on our honeymoon in Vienna during intermission at the opera.

Happily, life marched on. Alexei planted daffodils for me and black-eyed Susans for himself that we could watch grow in our pen-of-a-backyard from the window in the shower upstairs. My father and brothers and a cousin-in-law (three Joes among them) all helped us build the perfect deck out back, which Grandma, the family matriarch, blessed. It was in that little house where I think Alexei had one of his proudest married moments by giving his annoyingly observant wife a surprise thirtieth-birthday party. And less than a year later, so many of the same faces gathered again to wish us bon voyage as our young lives were headed for the Midwest, where Alexei would attend graduate art school and we'd plan our family.

I liked to tease Alexei about how it really was my breasts that got him into grad school. In the first semester of his senior year Alexei needed a subject for an art project. Then one night he looked at me curiously as I undressed before bed. "Your breasts are beautiful like Madonna's," he said. (She had just published her book *Sex.*)

I didn't need much more convincing than that to lend my anatomy to his artwork. What girl doesn't want to be an artist's muse? He greased up my body and then pressed me onto a lithograph stone. He did the same to himself and then merged the two images together on paper. The effect was an ethereal sensuousness.

Then, just a scant few months later, we started to have problems. Alexei was pulling away from me, but I could not understand why. He started spending more time at school. He would not come into the city to go out with me as much. The panic attacks to which he had always been prone came on more regularly. So we did what people do and sought counseling, and I hoped that our entwined hands would serve as comfort through the process.

In an effort to find something for us to do together I borrowed a jigsaw puzzle from my parents and set it up on the dining room table. For a few weeks we worked on it together listening to new music Alexei picked up at the record store. But he lost interest and I finished the puzzle alone on nights when he was at class. We started to go to therapy separately. Then, on a very uneventful day after a very uneventful commute back from the city and a very uneventful walk home down Main Street, I opened the door to our little house and found Alexei sitting in our overstuffed Ikea chair crying. He had had a breakthrough in therapy.

Nothing prepared me for what he said next: he'd been sexually abused as a child by a male friend of the family. The therapy helped him a lot but did little for me. During one solo session the therapist actually told me I looked cute when I cried. I didn't mention this to Alexei because I wanted him to continue with the therapy that seemed to be bringing him back to himself—and to us.

When his acceptance to grad school arrived, it meant a move to Michigan, and I wasn't sure I wanted to leave my job in New York. Oddly enough, my oldest sister was planning a big move to Oklahoma with her husband and three small children that summer. The morning after her going-away party—a backyard affair with friends and family and kids tossing water balloons—I woke up and declared to Alexei that we needed to go to Michigan together.

We talked it all out that morning. "What about your job?" he asked. I couldn't believe he could know me so well and not know that family came first. "You and me, that's our family," I told him. "A writer can write anywhere, but being together and planning for our family, that we could only do together—whether in Michigan or anywhere else." We'd rent out the house and return, or not, after graduate school, depending on where the opportunities led us. After that, I never had any doubts about leaving New York. My assurance and our commitment buoyed him, and a renewed excitement filled the air around us as we made plans for our midwestern adventure. When Alexei stopped going to therapy I didn't object because we were back in sync with each other.

Everything fell into place after that. When I told my magazine editor that I was moving to Michigan she said, "Oh, damn!" But, as it turned out, she needed a new midwestern correspondent. So Alexei would get his degree and I'd stay connected to my world, too.

Our friends and family helped us pack our belongings into a U-Haul and we spent the last night in our little house sleeping on our mattress on the living room floor. Our best friends, Eli and Eva, made the trip with us. We communicated by walkie-talkie, the girls in the Volkswagen and the boys in the truck. A few hours into the trip, when I pulled the sun visor down, an envelope dropped into my lap and I handed it to Eva.

"It's money," she said.

"What?"

Then she read the note: "Do something fun in Michigan." I easily recognized my brother Patrick's handwriting. He must have snuck into the car sometime while we were busy packing.

"That's so Patrick," I said, with a few tears in my eyes. We were off on our adventure with my family's blessing and a couple extra hundred dollars, too.

And so, Michigan.

Living at Cranbrook is like living in an art Disneyland. It was originally the country estate of George and Ellen Scripps Booth, she of the Scripps newspaper wealth that he eventually took over. Named for the English village from which the Booth family hailed, by the 1920s Cranbrook had established itself as a center of the American arts and crafts movement. Forty acres of gardens surround the manor house, which now serves as the administrative hub of the six institutions the Booths founded on its grounds: a children's school, separate boys' and girls' middle schools, an Episcopal church, a science institute, and a graduate arts school. Eliel Saarinen designed many of the buildings constructed on the campus during the 1920s through the 1940s. Evidence that the sculptor Carl Milles once resided at Cranbrook is found in his work that pops up all over the grounds.

We rented an apartment on the top floor of a two-story carriage house attached to a larger apartment building called Hedgegate. Our kitchen occupied the space above the connecting archway between the two buildings constructed in 1927 by an architect named L. J. Heenan. By 1994, when we moved in, ivy climbed up the whitewashed walls. My favorite architectural elements were the windows—the thick, multipaned, lead-glass variety that opened out. I set up my home office in the slanted space beneath a dormer on one of side of the living room.

Quickly we made friends with Mitch and Sally, who lived together upstairs in the bigger building. As with Eli and Eva, we felt at home in each other's apartments and ping-ponged back and forth easily for parties or just late nights talking and drinking as art students will do. It's the closest we'd ever come to being bohemians.

A married couple, Alexei and I were an anomaly at grad school, but we didn't care. We even decided that we'd try to get pregnant during the second semester—we were back on track, perhaps even closer than ever. We joked about who would be the godparents and how we could play our upstairs friends against our best friends at home. We teased Eli and Eva about Mitch and Sally when we visited New Jersey for Christmas. Once, on that holiday, we even made love in the car on a secluded street by the beach, because the pullout couches we slept on at our friends' and relatives' houses provided very little privacy. We were young and in love.

But when the next semester started, Alexei's artwork took on darker and darker elements in both theme and color. One Sunday at Mass, when the priest was talking about how Cardinal Bernardin of Chicago forgave the man who had falsely accused him of molestation, Alexei walked out in the middle of the sermon. I made an appointment with the priest the next day, and he gave me the name of a therapist, Ron. Just in time, I thought, because my husband was disappearing before my eyes again.

Our upstairs friends didn't suspect anything was wrong at first, because Alexei and I always played well together and truly loved each other's company. We continued to go to "lounge"—a twice-weekly grad school event that turned a room in the basement of the art museum on campus into a bar complete with music and dancing. We even went sledding in the campus gardens with Mitch and Sally in the wee hours of the morning.

Still, Alexei went to his studio earlier and earlier and came home later and later. I knew I was drinking too much and started racewalking in the mornings to work out my frustrations. We continued therapy with Ron. Alexei placed lavender around the apartment because Ron said the scent might help boost his sex drive. It didn't help. We weren't having sex very often, if at all.

During Lent I started going to church every morning like I had with my mother before I started first grade. You'd think a five-year-old would dread daily Mass, but being there with my mother basking in the peaceful presence she emanated during her daily personal communion with God transformed church—and really all religious ceremony—into a lifelong source of comfort for me. And I needed comfort. I wished I could talk with my mother about Alexei and our troubles, but I didn't feel that I could. It would be unfair to Alexei.

Therapy helped, but I really didn't understand what I was dealing with until I happened to meet a small publisher on a business trip to Traverse City. I addressed a group of publishers in what turned out to be a very small informal setting in a non-descript hotel conference room. The group included about a half dozen members of a local publishers association, and when we went around the room introducing ourselves one of the women said she was a psychologist who specialized in childhood sexual abuse. I thought, here's God putting someone in my path again.

Back home, I waited for Alexei to go to his studio and then I called the woman. I told her what was happening with me and Alexei and immediately felt a wave of relief at just saying the words out loud to someone other than Ron. She advised me to read a book called *Courage to Heal.* Before I read the book I had had a hard time imagining what was going through Alexei's mind as he grappled with the reality of his abuse. He certainly didn't want to talk about it with me.

In my next solo session with Ron I told him that the book really helped. He was surprised I hadn't read it before, because he'd advised Alexei to read it and he even had Alexei doing some exercises from a complementary workbook. At first I felt betrayed by being left out of what Alexei was going through, but then Ron helped me understand that I needed to respect the privacy of Alexei's psyche. "Even in therapy it happens; someone will have a breakthrough in one session and then pull back the next couple of meetings," Ron offered. "All you can do is love him—and I know you are doing that."

Hold on to my hand, Alexei, please, I'd pray in church.

Then one day while I was driving along in our Volkswagen listening to a new mixed tape Alexei had made, a song I had never heard before by Matthew Sweet came on and the lyrics stung me. I pulled over and listened again and again. He sang about wanting someone to pull the trigger and shoot him: "This hole in my heart's getting bigger / Everything I'll ever be, I've been." I knew in that instant that Alexei wanted to let go of my hand.

Even now the smell of lavender can bring me to tears.

One June, I went to Chicago on a business trip for a weekend and Alexei went to Maine to visit his family for a few weeks. Shortly after I returned I received a letter postmarked from Maine. "Hi dear. How you doing? Miss me?" it started. "I don't really have a whole lot to tell you but I felt like writing." He was staying with his sister and brother-in-law and their two sons on their small farm. He wrote about watching movies on cable and how they all went to bed by ten. He said he had some good talks with his sister, but I knew he didn't talk about his abuse because he didn't want to tell anyone about that. "I'll probably call you today and tell you the same things," he wrote. "Love you & see you soon, Alexei."

As luck would have it, the husband of a woman I met at church was away at precisely the same time as Alexei. So Lorraine invited me over for a beer. She and her husband were art collectors and gave a lot of their money to Cranbrook. They liked to entertain art students, so this was not my first time in Lorraine and Henry's eclectically decorated living room. When we settled down with our beers, I asked how she and Henry met.

"Boy, you sure can ask 'em," Lorraine said. I thought it was a simple and obvious question.

As it turned out, Lorraine got pregnant when she was a young woman in her native Paris. She knew the baby's father wasn't going to be reliable and so she decided to have the child on her own. She got a job teaching art history and a few years later asked a colleague to father another child for her. She planned to remain a single parent. The night she gave birth in her home, friends and colleagues gathered downstairs to celebrate. Henry was one of the guests.

Both of their sons had come to visit their parents while we were at Cranbrook, and I never would have guessed that Henry was not their biological father. Lorraine never actually said these words, but the lesson I took away that night was that marriages and families were always complicated, and happily-ever-afters are not always what you think they will be. With my marriage falling apart all around me, the lesson came just in time. Maybe Alexei and I still could find a way to hold on; maybe we needed an unconventional way of working things out. I would have done almost anything.

When Alexei got back, we were both ready to talk seriously about what we were going to do. He said he felt guilty because he wasn't taking care of me at all. We cried and together decided that it might make sense if I moved to Chicago, where I'd have more access to work-related activities and give him the room to finish the second year of grad school without feeling so guilty about me. I said I wouldn't go until the end of the summer. Somehow summer alone seemed too much to bear.

We hung out with Mitch and Sally; by now, we had told them about our problems. I encouraged Alexei to be honest at least with them. We all swam together in the man-made lake on campus. We went dancing at a cheesy local hotel lounge that had an equally cheesy lounge singer. Alexei helped me pack. I remember we drank wine and laughed as we negotiated who got which CDs like trading baseball cards.

Alexei and I went to Chicago for a weekend to find an apartment. The places the Realtor showed us were depressing, and I had almost given up until we walked by a garden-style apartment building with a "for rent" sign planted among the gladiolas in the courtyard. We celebrated the find with a fancy dinner at a sidewalk café at our hotel. Alexei told me he was glad we had gotten our friendship back that summer. I wanted to scream, "I don't want a friend! I want my HUSBAND!" But I can't remember if I said anything. The important things in life never feel like they are happening.

Lorraine and Henry gave me a farewell barbecue. Then, on the Friday before Labor Day, Mitch and Sally helped us move our furniture to Chicago, the girls in the Volkswagen and the boys in the U-Haul. This time there was no Patrick envelope tucked away in the visor. Mitch and Sally gave Alexei and me time alone and we sat on the back stairs—Chicago apartments always seem to have back stairs—and cried and cried.

"I want you to call me sometime when you have the kitchen door open and I can hear the rain out here," he said. I remembered waking up in the middle of a thunderstorm and sharing a Klondike bar snuggled in bed in our little house. Mitch and

Alexei returned the truck the next day. Alexei and I hugged and kissed and said "I love you," and then the three of them left.

I stood and watched our little Volkswagen go down Broadway and turn onto Addison. I heard the spring on the courtyard gate uncoil with a soft screech as I opened it and walked into the plush green and flowery courtyard. I heard it bang shut as I made my way down the sidewalk to my apartment in the back of the two-story U-shaped brick building. The phone company was sending someone out on Tuesday, so I had no phone for three days. Victor, the only friend I had in Chicago, was away, so alone and with nothing to do but cry, I manically unpacked and set up house. I called my parents and Alexei collect from the pay phone in front of the grocery store next door.

We said we'd work on our marriage long distance, but that didn't happen. We spoke often, but Alexei wouldn't talk about therapy, or us, or anything, really. I didn't feel like I should pressure him. He came to visit for my birthday in October and we held hands as we explored my new neighborhood together. He talked about school. I talked about work and the people I was meeting. We ran into Victor on Clark Street, and he suggested we go to a nearby bar. The three of us drank and laughed and played pinball. "This wasn't as awkward as I thought it might be," Alexei said the next morning over coffee.

Again, I can't remember what I said; I am sure I said something about how our having fun together was never a problem. We held hands easily, we kissed hello and good-bye, but that was all the intimacy Alexei would allow. I tried to find out how his therapy was going, but he didn't want to talk about it. "Alexei, you can't shut me out," I must have said. My journal from that year is empty from my birthday through Thanksgiving, when I visited Alexei in Michigan.

I arrived late at night at what was once our apartment, which Alexei now shared with a roommate. He averted my kiss. He had set up his room in what was our living room and gotten a kitten. I tried not to think of the significance of his getting a cat when I never wanted any pets. Perhaps the kitten was good therapy, I told myself. We spent Thanksgiving at Mitch and Sally's and one of our other friends came by later. We all played charades. Pictures from that night show Mitch and me dancing around with sparklers.

At lunch the next day, Sally told me that Alexei wanted to really talk with me but he was afraid. She didn't know more than that. She came with me to Alexei's new studio; I was dying to see what he'd been working on. Bob, Alexei's new studio-mate, was a slob, and I was surprised that Alexei could work in such a mess. Working with found objects had always been of interest to him, but the place looked like Sanford and Son's storage room. I didn't see any of Alexei's work around, and when I asked about it, he begrudgingly took out some large abstract paintings. He didn't bother explaining any of it to me, and I didn't think he wanted to hear my questions. I felt smacked in the face and I just wanted to run out of there with Sally and cry. But Mitch showed up, and he wanted me to see what he had been working on. So we all went to Mitch's studio, where he bubbled over with words about his work.

Eventually Alexei and I went back to the apartment. We lay down beneath the dormer on his futon that smelled of cat. When I started crying, "the talk" began. For the first time in my life, when I looked into Alexei's eyes I couldn't read them.

He told me that he couldn't be married to anyone. Something was broken inside of him, he said, and he didn't know if he could ever fix it. He wanted to go away. When I asked him where he'd like to go, he said Austria, "because that's where we were." I couldn't understand. The man I had loved for eight years had just told me he couldn't be married to anyone and yet he wanted to escape to where we spent our honeymoon? I cried myself to sleep that night and was grateful that I would be leaving in the morning. He gave me nothing. Not even a reason. What happened to my husband? Who was this man who called himself Alexei and occupied his body and looked at me blankly with those amber-hazel eyes that once desired me so much?

I know I went temporarily insane when I returned to the limbo that was Chicago, but somehow I managed to work. I wrote to Ron back in Michigan, who just the summer before had assured me that my moving was not a desertion of my marriage. "Sometimes when people have been traumatized they hold onto the pain because it is what is familiar to them," he told me. "Some people won't let themselves be happy." I couldn't comprehend it. "I'm afraid that Bridget is going to take care of everybody else but Bridget," he said. He tried to encourage me to permit myself to envision a life with someone else. When Ron wrote back to me, he ended his letter with this: "Flash that amazing smile of yours and let Chicago know you've been there."

So I tried my best to pull my chin up and get to work. But sometimes I couldn't hide myself, and the confusion I felt about everything, well enough. Once it happened when I was working on a profile of a local poet who started a poetry slam at the Green Mill, a legendary bar in the Uptown part of the city. The poet, Marc Smith, asked me if I had any requests for him to perform that night, and I asked him to read a poem he wrote called "My Father's Coat," a raw and bitter account of a brutal father's legacy revealed to the son as he wore the old woolen hand-me-down. Smith shot me a quizzical look. "I'm not thinking of my father," I assured him.

After the slam I sat down with Smith and one of his friends, two guys in their forties I assumed had done a lot of living in Chi-town. As I conducted the interview, Smith was playful and even a little flirty with me, which I found unnerving, not because I was insulted but because I didn't know how to handle myself anymore as a woman. If my marriage was really over, did that make me single? The tears came faster than I could excuse myself from the table. I knew they saw them. I went to the ladies' room and composed myself. Back at the table I apologized.

"I just recently separated from my husband and I don't understand anything, and everything feels raw," I told them.

Smith put his hand on top of mine, glanced at his friend, and then fixed his eyes on mine with a rather fatherly expression. "We were just saying that it is so rare to see anyone have a true emotion," he said. Then we ordered drinks.

That's how it went for me those first lonely months of uncertainty in Chicago. For the most part I held myself together but sometimes the simmering feelings were too powerful to conceal. Not everyone was fooled by my bubbly exterior, which wasn't really an act so much as my relying on my nature to pull me through. Once, when I stopped by a bookstore in the Loop to drop off the magazine that featured a profile I had written about the proprietor, the octogenarian Stuart Brent saw right through me. I told him briefly what had happened. By way of an answer he grabbed a copy of *The Little Prince* off a shelf and read me a passage from it. I can't remember which passage he read, but I will never forget what he said after that: "There is no past and no future right now, only the present."

A few minutes later his old friend Studs Terkel came into the store, and the three of us sat at the round oak table in the back, where it was obvious they had spent many a day together. I listened to the old men tell their stories. Before I left, Studs Terkel took my hand, leaned in, pointed at me, and said, "Yooou've got something."

Yeah, I thought, walking down Michigan Avenue afterward, what do I do with it now?

Seven months after Thanksgiving in Michigan Alexei came to Chicago to tell me he thought he was gay.

In an instant everything I thought I knew changed forever and eviscerated even the memories. The only thing I do remember from this conversation is that it was as if it had nothing to do with me. Alexei only talked about himself and his pain. In those moments, I was too broken and stunned to think clearly. Now, when I remember this pivotal moment in my life, all I see is the illumination of the antique iron reading lamp Alexei bought for his bookish wife. On a stool beneath its glow stood the Underwood typewriter from the front porch of my parents' house on Main Street. As a girl I used to move chess pieces, black for the men and white for the women, up the "steps" of the typewriter for an imaginary royal wedding.

My present, such as it was, provided little comfort.

Alexei let go of my hand, moved on into a life we had planned together in another city where he had no past, and never really looked back. I tried to look forward without him.

I got involved way too soon with a truly wonderful man who loved me madly. I wasn't ready for it. So at thirty-three, the year after the divorce, I got accepted into Columbia's Graduate School of Journalism and I moved to New York. An escape? Probably.

But it brought me back near my family and, if it was an escape, at least it would be a constructive one. It seemed like a good way to jump-start my reentry into my own life. Some people seek therapy; others earn graduate degrees.

Actually, I did see a therapist, but she was one of those who parroted back everything I said to her. "So, you say you feel disconnected . . ." It didn't do much good. Exercise helped. Ironically, on those days when I felt especially run-down from journalism boot camp and got to feeling especially sorry for myself about the divorce, wouldn't you know it, God or fate or whatever would throw this three-legged dog in my path in the park as if to mock me and say, "So, you think *you're* pathetic?" And I'd lighten up. To top it off, I had heard the dog's owner call her "Bridy," the traditional Irish nickname for Bridget that one of my magazine editors called me when he was being playful.

At my saddest moments I instinctively look for such distractive graces. In the years after the divorce I did so many things to distract myself from the pain. I spent a month in Rome, where I discovered I could feel joy again. In New York I enjoyed the company of an urban tribe of friends. I dove into my work at the magazine, where I became the editor of my own section. I dated a few men who just couldn't deal with the arsenal of hurt that came with me. Who could blame them?

I swallowed myself up and tried to enjoy my family. But some things just get to you. One evening, after spending the day with my brother Joseph's family in New Jersey, I hung around to help him and his wife put their four children to bed. As I was closing the bathroom door so that my five-year-old niece would not feel a draft while her father bathed her, I heard her ask in her squeaky, little-kid voice: "Is Aunt Bridget lonely?"

"Why do you say that, sweetie?" my brother asked.

"Because she has no babies."

Yes, sweetie, your aunt Bridget's lonely, I thought, with tears spilling down my face. Deep breath. Deep breath. On my way back to Brooklyn I drove by the Garden State Parkway exit for the town where Alexei and I once owned our little house. I knew that the road sign for Metuchen and my niece's question shouldn't make me hurt so much, but they did.

Like Alexei, I needed to start life over again in a place where I had no past.

My editor said "Oh, damn!" again when I told her I wanted to move. She suggested California, where I could keep my hand in things as *Publishers Weekly*'s West Coast correspondent. So I packed up again and held a stoop sale where I sold many of the things that reminded me of the past. I threw out my wedding shoes and my divorce dress in the same Hefty bag.

My family supported my decision even if they didn't want me to move so far away. My parents and my siblings came into New York for a good-bye bash I coordinated for my publishing friends. My astrologer friend Susan Miller did people's charts on her laptop. One slightly older male colleague told my father that if his twelve-year-old daughter turned out to be a woman like me, he'd be proud. Then a hush came over the room when Jane Friedman, the CEO of HarperCollins, dropped by to toast me and my new adventure. "You've got to meet my mom," I blurted out when I approached her. And Jane kindly assured my parents that the employees at her San Francisco office would see to it that I wasn't completely alone out there. "I have grown children, too," she told my mom. "And I don't know what I'd do if one of them moved so far away."

This time I hired movers. Then I drove to South Jersey, where my parents planned a family farewell in the backyard of their home in a retirement community. The locals call these homes "poodle" houses because they are small and so well groomed.

When I got up in the morning, my mother had already finished her prayers and was sitting on the couch with a coffee cup. She came into her sparkling clean blue-and-white kitchen and sat at the counter as I poured some coffee for myself. My mom had made Grandma's biscotti for my farewell dunking.

My mother and I have always communicated well, even when I was a little girl. Perhaps youngest children are spoiled most with the luxury of time alone with their moms. In the mornings we had church, then I'd follow mom around as she cleaned every day. On special days we'd go out to lunch, just the two of us mostly, but sometimes with one of her friends.

The Molly Pitcher Inn on the Navesink River in Red Bank was my favorite place. In the first grade I feigned sick once because I missed my lunches with Mom, and she went along with the ruse. "Well, honey," she said after she picked me up from school, smelling always of Arpege, "I hope you are going to be well enough to have lunch with Mrs. Keggly." We didn't drink soda often in my family, but that day my mom ordered me a Coke because the syrup might be good for my tummy.

I remembered how before I made my move to Chicago, I had visited my parents alone in their poodle house. We spent several nights sitting at the counter in their spotless kitchen while I tried to explain to them what was happening in my marriage. Alexei had been sexually abused, and he built a wall around himself and wouldn't let me in. My mother wanted him to come there and stay with them awhile so she could mother him. My father, for whom the very idea of a man molesting a boy caused nausea, tried to be sympathetic with Alexei. "But there comes a time when you have to shit or get off the pot," he said.

Ever gentler than my dad, my mom took me to lunch at Molly Pitcher's. The sight of a mother with her little girl at a table near the window started my tears again. I had been so confused and alone with Alexei's secret. I didn't want to move and leave Alexei behind. I wanted to take care of him. "You never left Daddy," I said, knowing that my parents had had their own difficulties, not that I ever really knew what they were even as an adult.

"Don't you do that," my mother snapped, her voice taking on a gentle sharpness. "Don't compare your life to anyone else's—not even mine. I had five children." For better or worse my parents weathered their storms, and what my mother was trying to teach me that day at lunch was that every husband and wife faced challenges and ultimately had to figure out what was best for them. If I thought moving to Chicago would give Alexei the chance to work toward healing himself then that's what I should do.

Now here I was back again sitting in my mom's sparkling kitchen talking about another move, this time across the country. She knew why I was doing it, but I felt the need to explain again.

"It's days like today, Mom, that are the hardest," I said, anticipating the family gathering. "As much as I love them, and I know they love me, I get so envious that they got to have their families and I didn't. And I hate that. I don't want to be bitter." We both cried. We'd had this conversation before. "I never meant to move so far away, Mom, but . . ."

My tiny mother got up and hugged me, cradling my head at her chest. "Oh, Bridget, Bridget," I heard her say softly, as if praying over me. She rocked me. We cried a little, but not for long. "You'll start fresh in a place with no memories to haunt you."

By the time my father got up we were each on a third cup of coffee and, if a little jittery, composed again.

"What's going on in here?" he asked.

"Oh, you know, the talking, the crying," I said, but suddenly I didn't feel like crying anymore.

I enjoyed the party—and even playing with the kids. My cousin Renea, a mother of two, gave me a beautiful embroidered black shawl because she had read that San Francisco weather called for layers of clothing. My cousin Lisa, a mother of three, gave me a San Francisco guidebook and wrote, "Each day offers new opportunities and new beginnings. Take advantage of them all!" It's hard to feel bitter when people love you so much, but I knew that starting anew was still the thing to do.

The next morning, before I hopped in my little Cavalier to pick up my friend who was coming along on the cross-country trip, my mom gave me curtains she had made from old bed-sheets for my new bathroom window. Outside in the driveway my dad gave me a red rose from the yard, and I placed it on the dashboard. We hugged and shed a few tears, and then California there I went.

As in Chicago, the apartment-finding gods once again smiled upon me, and I settled into a sunny one-bedroom in a 1920s Spanish-style building on Merritt Avenue and Brooklyn in Oak-land. The building is situated on a hill in such a way that my desk facing the living room bay window landed at tree-top level with a pleasant view of Lake Merritt below. I called it my "tree house apartment" and took the Brooklyn/Merritt location as a good omen because I had just moved from Brooklyn and my dad's lawn mower shop of yore was named Merritt's.

California provided a clean slate, I hoped, but the thing about escape is that unless you deal with whatever you are escaping from, you never actually make the break. Others came to the Golden State to pan for gold, why couldn't I mine myself a new future? Settling into the new job was the easiest part. Jane Friedman's promise to my mother turned out to be right: the HarperSanFrancisco people did welcome me, and so did all of the Bay Area book community.

Californians love transplants and Californian publishing types particularly love transplants from New York. What made me even more intriguing to my new Western colleagues is the fact that I moved into my new life from New York on September 11, 2001. Just about a week after America's new day of infamy I found myself at a cocktail party at the Telegraph Hill home of Ann and Gordon Getty, known for their literary and other philanthropic interests.

Everyone seemed a little off balance. At first I wandered aimlessly around the party, admiring the fine antiques and art in the Gettys' drawing room and their magnificent view of San Francisco Bay. I remember finding it odd, the juxtaposition of all that opulence with the stark sight of Alcatraz on its island in the distance. I felt a little cast off in the water myself, but I should not have worried. The few people I had known in San Francisco from my many years in the book business quickly introduced me to others at the party; once I started meeting people it became clear that I was, indeed, a welcome newcomer.

Meeting Jack Jensen, the president of Chronicle Books, and his wife, Cathleen O'Brien, that night really stands out in my mind. You see, more than just welcoming me they wanted to know who I was and what I wanted to do with this new chapter of my life. And that's the way it went with many of the publishing people I met in the West: Yeah, sure, there's a job to do, but who are you?

Good question, but I wasn't quite ready to answer it. So I concentrated on work and began to make friends. A couple of my new friends even set me up on dates—they just couldn't figure out why a woman like me with so much to offer was alone. There was this cute guy, an entertainment lawyer about ten years older than me but still very hot, who took me out to dinner. It was pleasant enough and he drove us up to the Berkeley hills to show me the panoramic view of the Bay, its various bridges illuminating the night. He'd been divorced for years and had two daughters; his oldest had just started college. I dismissed my marriage with a few sentences: "I married a man who turned out to be gay. It was a whammy. It was also a long time ago. The best part about moving to California is that I have no history here." He pecked me on the cheek when he dropped me off at my tree house apartment. Nice guy.

We talked a few times on the phone. This was right about the time I began to hatch the idea that I might want to be a literary agent, and this guy could not have been more encouraging or helpful. Some of his clients were musicians and writers, so he knew of book contracts and he said that when the time came he'd be happy to take a look at anything my clients might have to sign. Generous, too.

The only problem was that by the time we had our second date, I knew it wasn't going to work out. It all came down to that old clincher—the kid issue. His girls were nearly grown and, while he was looking for a relationship, he wasn't looking to start another family. I was thirty-eight going on thirty-nine and, while I was trying to accept the fact that I might never have children, I didn't want to totally give up on it, either. He understood and was actually quite kind about it. We never dated again, but for a while he'd check in and see how I was doing as an agent and as someone making a new life for herself in a new land. He called me "intrepid."

Months later I met another man, another setup, for coffee, which seems to be what people do now on first dates. This guy was in his late forties and I can't remember what he did for a living, although I think it had something to do with computers. What stands out most is that he wanted children even more than I did—as impossible as that seemed, even to me. That's all he talked about. He remained friends with an ex-girlfriend's family and even went along with her sister and brother-in-law and their kids to Disneyland. The kids called him "Uncle." I stopped him from taking out his wallet and showing me pictures.

This guy had spent years trying to find a woman with whom he could have a family. He even went so far as to travel to Russia, where he met a young woman who wanted to come to America. In the end they wound up being just friends, and he actually helped put her through college in Russia. Another nice guy, but I couldn't help but think of that three-legged dog and how maybe this guy's obsession with children was a sign saying, "Relax, Bridget, you don't want to come across as that desperate."

Even if I was never going to see him again, I didn't dismiss his feelings. I knew where he was coming from, and he didn't even have the option of having a kid on his own, which is what some of my friends wanted me to consider. I felt bad for the guy, but I also had no desire to date him. As for having a kid on my own, as much as I respect other women who have taken that route, I knew it wasn't for me.

Rory's first letter arrived from prison about six months after my two setups and about six weeks before my thirty-ninth birthday. Working on Rory's book and the drama of both his backstory he revealed in his letters, and the horrible place from which he wrote them, all provided me with nice diversions.

That December I decided not to go to New Jersey for Christmas; I just couldn't bear the big family gathering. My family, being my family, understood. For the first time in my life my mother sent me a Mass card—she had arranged for a Mass to be said on Christmas Eve in Bethlehem for my intentions. Great, I thought, I'm so pathetic my mother is sending me Mass cards. Then I wondered if that was all I was going to get for Christmas, and I couldn't help but laugh at myself, a child still looking for presents under the tree on Christmas morning.

At about the same time, Rory sent me a letter that asked in a postscript (he loves postscripts):

> If you could go back, physically, to the day you made the worst decision of your life . . . a) Would you be able to convince the old you that you are the future you? . . . and b) Would you be able to make the younger you understand the consequences of her actions? Could you explain, get it through that young I-know-everything-mind? . . . and c) How would this one change in history affect the rest of the world? How far would the ripples reach from that one change?
> Please give this thought.
> Please answer me truthfully.
> This is my new novel.
> I'm going to change my entire life. (On paper at least ☺.)

In another postscript he begged me for a picture of myself, as he had in other letters. I decided to send him a picture, but I wasn't sure how to answer his questions. Was marrying Alexei the worst decision of my life? Would I believe myself if I tried to go back and warn my younger self about the consequences?

So I put on a Rosanne Cash CD and I sat down to write what turned out to be a very long letter. Up until that point I hadn't told Rory too much about my life. As I had been doing on dates, I brushed over my marriage and divorce—it is just so easy to fall in love with your own hard-luck story. But how could I answer Rory without telling him about all of *that*? Facing Rory's questions was already a depressing exercise; it being a few days before Christmas only made the task more emotionally charged. Still, I answered him and let the rawness of my feelings in writing out the past flow over me again.

No, I admitted, my young self wouldn't listen to my older self; however—and this is where it got really weird—I knew that if the older Alexei came to my young self I'd listen to him. What the heck did that mean? I dropped the questions from my head as I dropped my letter in the mailbox. I had enough on my mind facing Christmas alone without thinking about that too much.

Then fate stepped in again. Out of the blue, my youngest cousin, Karen, who was in grad school in Georgia (the one who played the oboe at my wedding), sent me an e-mail saying that she and her husband, Jeremy, were spending the holidays with Jeremy's parents at their home on the border of Napa and Sonoma counties. She knew it was last minute, and the only night she had free was Christmas Eve, but did I want to come and spend the night with them? Karen and her family are Jewish, so what she offered me wasn't a Christmas party, although she said her father-in-law had joked that with me under their roof Santa just might show up.

In a way, he did, because there, without warning, I had the family gathering I longed for but couldn't face back home. It was

Christmas without all the trimmings, but without all the baggage as well. (My mom did send me a Christmas present besides the Mass card.)

Karen's in-laws were incredibly welcoming. We ate tuna steaks, drank great wine, and talked about everything from politics to books until late at night. I never heard Santa's sleigh bells, but sitting with Jeremy's mom talking over coffee the next morning one-on-one was the perfect Christmas present. When I told my mom about this later, I knew she was glad that I had found a surrogate, at least for Christmas morning.

Then there was the added present of catching up with Karen, who was the happiest I had ever seen her. Karen was about four when her mother and my uncle fell in love, bringing Aunt Jan and Karen and her slightly older brother, Daniel, into our lives. I had brought a picture taken the first summer Uncle Drew brought them along to the lakeside cabin my parents rented every year in Cooperstown, New York. I was fourteen, and the photo shows me kneeling down and wrapping a towel around a wet, shivering Karen with her little-kid belly sticking out of a blue one-piece bathing suit. What Karen remembered most about joining our family was the culture shock. My aunt Jan is English and an only child who didn't have much of an extended family. Their father's family was small, too, so Karen and Daniel didn't know what to expect when they joined a brood like ours. "I just remember being in your backyard and Patrick and Joseph tossing me around," said Karen. "That would be my brothers," I answered.

What I remembered most from that first Cooperstown with Karen was when my uncle Drew, my godfather who just happened to carry around my kindergarten picture in his wallet, took it out and compared it with Karen's preschool photo. In

our Celtic features—the freckles, the light hair, the blue eyes—
you could almost see a family resemblance. Blood or not, years
of Sunday dinners at Grandma's, holidays, weddings, and the
most multiethnic bar mitzvah and bat mitzvah I had ever attended, made us family.

But the best Christmas present of all was the flight of bitterness I felt leaving my heart as I honestly hoped without any envy
that everything would work out for Karen and Jeremy, the newlyweds. It's hokey, but I returned to my apartment with a renewed sense of peace on earth and goodwill toward men. Even
though I had not heard back from Rory, I sent him another letter, a happier letter. Our letters overlapped, and right after New
Year's I received his reply to my attempt to answer his young
self/old self riddle. He wrote:

> When it rains here, for days and days, as it has now, the
> cell turns cold. The air grows thick and moist. And the con-
> crete walls, which confine me, they begin to sweat.
>
> I am aware that this is not a phenomenon that it is eas-
> ily explained away by the laws of physics/metaphysics/sci-
> ence, but I still choose to believe that it is special, unique,
> that the walls which hold me captive are crying the tears
> which I so often swallow down a throat constricted by emo-
> tions I cannot show.
>
> You see, in here there is no crying.
>
> Emotion, anything but hate-rage-violence, will be
> taken as a sign of weakness, will be taken advantage of.
>
> Yet, halfway through your letter, Bridget, I was forced to
> put it down, to lie out on my bunk and face the wall, to cry
> with it, because I could no longer keep them from spilling.
>
> When my celly asked me what I was doing, I was silent.

He let me be, an un-communicated understanding for which I was grateful.

If I would've spoken, the dam would have broken.

I speak of this without embarrassment or pride, Bridget. I am telling you this only because it is real, this effect you have had on me, this change you have caused in me. For to even glimpse the smallest piece of a soul bared, as I feel you have done for me with your own, is to truly befriend another. It is to share life. To share, to intoxicate another with the same chemicals of sorrow or joy, of loss or gain, to reproduce such a subtle nuance as personal emotion, as you have done, it is the most amazing feat of human relationships.

He went on to tell me that this connection is much more fulfilling and powerful than sex. Rory always managed to bring sex in somewhere in his letters, which I tried to overlook. He continued to address my letter:

Poor Alexei. Loving. Funny. Damaged.

I feel his pain even more so, and therefore your burden of loving him, yet I could not shed one tear for him. Because, to answer your implied question, the one you hoped I could not imagine, I have and I can. For I am also a child of the secret . . .

I hope he learns to forgive.

I hope he learns to not let it define him.

You know what is funny, not really funny, really sad actually, is that we are shaped more by the things we survive than the things we enjoy. Why is that so?

Since other eyes read all correspondence in and out of prison, you have to be careful how you word things; with "a child of the secret," Rory had just subtly revealed to me that he had been sexually abused. That bit of information in the wrong hands could be used against him. There can be no weakness in prison, remember? But then aren't all children of the secret silenced? As collateral damage, wasn't I silenced as well? Even within my close and loving family, few knew the real initial cause of my and Alexei's marital difficulties. I read on:

Bridget, you asked me if I have 'ever been happy in love?'

And how can I answer that without sounding utterly pathetic? Because the truth is that my heart has always been my downfall. I am too honest, too emotional, too loyal. I am a recovering romantic addict who still hopes to be proven wrong. Pathetically, I still hope to find that special someone and live happily ever after.

I know, stupid me, right?

To answer your question, yes. Too many times. I am one of those stupid men that will stand up and sing a love song to you in the middle of a crowded restaurant, massage your feet and paint your toe nails while we watch an old black-and-white movie on a Saturday morning, send you flowers at work for no other reason than to think that other people should see your real smile.

What an idiot, right?

Oh, believe me, I am such the fool. I think you know how this worked out for me. It led to pain every single time. It would crush me every single time, that nobody ever felt it quite as strong, that eventually they would move on, leaving me aching-sobbing-wondering what more I could have done to help them feel what I had in my heart.

Then Rory said good night and took a break because it was too painful for him to write anything else. He started fresh on the next page, having slept and gone to "R&R," receiving and release, where he picked up the package of books I had sent him for Christmas. This improved his spirits greatly and he thanked me profusely. He ended the letter with just one more thing he had to say: "As I continue to write and grow as a person, I will be able to reach much higher. For I am determined to get better, to someday become something special and amazing. With your help and friendship, this will happen." Then he signed off with "Tears and Smiles."

Rory's letters always came back to hope, and it impressed me how he managed to find it even while locked away for life in the most hopeless place. So with his cue, I took "Tears and Smiles" as my theme for the New Year—to tackle tears and search for more smiles.

CHAPTER 4

HURRICANES AND EARTHQUAKES

The drive to prison always starts with prison. It's hard not to eye San Quentin, which stands at the foot of the Marin Headlands, as I make my way across the Richmond Bridge on the first leg of the seven-hour trip. The early afternoon sun hits the razor wire of its death fences, glittering as if in motion with the waves of the sea. Whenever I go over any of the bridges that span across the San Francisco Bay I almost always pause and think about what a beautiful place I live in—beautiful and dangerous. Perhaps beauty and danger are never really far apart.

The unseen danger here lies deep within the earth. Anyone who moves from the East to the West Coast and says they are not afraid of earthquakes is lying. I grew up with the threat of hurricanes. Hurricanes I understand. They come with warning. They last hours. Sometimes they blow over with hardly a whimper, but as those poor souls on the Gulf Coast learned all too well, hurricanes kill. I've never experienced a truly devastating hurricane, but a few years before I was born one named Donna tore up most of the Atlantic seaboard, including the Jersey shore. My Irish grandfather's miniature train ride on the boardwalk at the edge of my hometown was destroyed. My parents kept pictures of Donna's devastation in a drawerful of family memories in my father's dresser. Recently, my parents did a little housecleaning and dispersed the pictures to me and my siblings.

Eleven photos from my portion of the Kinsella archives sit in a Ziploc bag inside the suitcase I'd packed for my impromptu escape up to visit Rory on a bright Friday morning the last weekend in August. Sometimes I wish that I was not so cognizant of the calendar. Certain dates just stay with me. Say, for instance, I planned a meeting on September 28, I'd think "Claire's birthday" (my sister), and it'd be a knee-jerk kind of thing. The last weekend in August was when Alexei and I got engaged on Martha's Vineyard. I don't need a psychologist to tell me that I was avoiding the memory of that event by taking a road trip on this particular weekend thirteen years later.

Was Rory my latest distraction? Since we'd opened ourselves up to each other post-Christmas he had become a huge source of comfort. I knew I had become the same for him. If anything, I thought that I would be the one doing the helping and I didn't see any danger in that. Besides, I just wanted to get outside of my own head for a while, so why not go to prison?

The entire summer I had been obsessed with the reality of turning forty in October and trying to come to terms with the fact that I would probably never have children. My friends tried to tell me I still had plenty of time. Their encouragement provided little comfort and it just wasn't true—at least not for me. Sure, women had babies in their forties all the time. My own grandmother had a daughter at forty-four. One option, the sperm-bank route, just wasn't for me. Adoption? Maybe down the road, but for now I needed to mourn the loss of what I had wanted. Nobody wanted to let me do that.

It's human nature for people to encourage others to hold on to hope. But the hope of motherhood was strangling me and I knew it. Why was it so hard for others to hear me say the truth I needed to voice? When Alexei and I first divorced, I was stunned by how many people felt perfectly comfortable saying, "At least you didn't have children." What is this compulsion we have for bright-siding other people's pain? A few times I retorted, "And I may never have any children now," and made a quick getaway from a person who was only trying to be positive. Of all the things such bright-siders said, the one that irked me the most was when people with children tried to tell me that having children was not the central defining event of their lives. It always made me feel a little sorry for their kids.

As obsessed as I am with being childless, I do not romanticize parenthood. On Sunday mornings, when I have undisturbed hours to read the papers and drink way too much coffee, with hardly even a phone call to interrupt me, I think of how my sister-in-law with four small children would probably give just about anything for even a half hour of such peace. Her days are dictated by carpools and sports schedules, whereas I can do whatever I want with my time.

My thoughts also drift to Sunday mornings as a child in the house on Main Street. Always an early riser, I often happened upon my mother alone reading the paper on the enclosed and many-windowed front porch. She'd be in her pajamas, a real coffee cup, the delicate kind with a saucer, resting on the seat cushion next to her on the wicker couch. I'd make tea and grab the funnies. We didn't talk much on such mornings, but, oh, the sense of contentment we shared in simply breathing the same air, feeling the same early-morning sunshine on our skin. I think of moments like this when I wonder what it must feel like to place your first child in the hands of the woman whose mere presence means comfort and peace.

Maybe if I hadn't had such beautiful maternal role models I would not have wanted to be a mother so much myself. I try to warn myself against the dangers of nostalgia—there is no guarantee that I would even be a good mother, but I am kind of sure I would.

With all this talk about biological clocks, I think something gets lost. I don't want a child because I think I need that to fully be a woman. I just can't fathom not experiencing that kind of love. But rather than listen to childless people whine about being childless, society wants us to buck up and bear it.

I tried to squelch the fear of childlessness as the years ticked by, but facing forty made that impossible.

Of course, the media doesn't help, either.

"Having a baby changes everything," that's what the Johnson & Johnson television commercial says. Ouch go the ovaries. I knew I had become a cliché—divorced and devastated and facing childlessness at forty. Even I grew tired of my whining. When I found myself barking "Shut up!" at the TV every time the next Hollywood mom-to-be was featured on some program, I thought a little escape couldn't hurt.

That spring I had the opportunity to interview many authors, but the conversation I remembered most was when I spoke with Marlo Thomas. She had just edited a book called *The Right Words at the Right Time*—a collection of essays penned by famous people (Al Pacino, Ruth Bader Ginsburg, Gwyneth Paltrow among them) about when someone said the exact thing they needed to hear at a precise moment in their lives. When Thomas was first starting out as an actress, her father sent her a present on the opening night of a play. Inside the box were horse blinders and a note that read, "Run your own race, baby!"

Admittedly, I was enamored with Ms. Thomas before the interview even happened. What American girl growing up in the late sixties/early seventies didn't want to be part Ann Marie, part Mary Richards—if for their wardrobe alone? They were so much more than TV characters; they were strong, independent, and very feminine women. Marlo Thomas could not have been any more gracious on the phone. When she asked me what were the right words said to me at the right time, I told her about my grandmother.

During the spring semester at Columbia I took the equipment I had for my radio journalism workshop with me to visit my grandmother in Orange, New Jersey. I had started to tape our conversations for posterity. Grandma was ninety-five at the time. Coming from such a big family, rarely was I spoiled enough to have Grandma all to myself, but on one warm spring day in 1998 Grandma and I sat in her kitchen and talked and talked. She said that when she first spotted my grandfather back at a party in their Italian village she said to herself that he was the one she'd marry. "But I no tell nobody," she said, her rheumy eyes filled with joy and her words flavored with the dialect of her region.

Even though Grandpa had been gone for more than a decade, Grandma always pointed toward his chair at the table when she talked about him. Grandpa got up every day and rode the bus into Manhattan, where he set up his shoe-shining stand in front of the building that housed the Chubb Insurance Company. Eventually Mr. Chubb got to know my grandfather and invited him into the building to shine shoes. Although he was never an employee of the company, "Andy," as everyone called him, was written up in the company newsletter. Whenever Chubb got rid of its old office furniture my grandfather took some pieces home, which is how I came to write on an old Chubb Insurance desk. Upon his "retirement" Mr. Chubb presented my grandfather with a pension, which my grandmother still lived on.

"Grandpa was happy," I said to my grandmother.

"Happiness, you make them" was her reply. My right words at the right time, I told Ms. Thomas during the interview, now several years after Grandma's death.

"With her accent and broken English she misspoke, making happiness plural," I explained to Ms. Thomas. "And I like that, because it is good to be reminded that happiness is not just one thing and is always of your making."

Seated at my Chubb desk the next day, I nearly fell off my chair when I answered the phone and Marlo Thomas's voice said hello. "What was it that your grandmother said again?" she asked. "I was going to tell someone about this thing my friend's Italian grandmother told her, but I couldn't remember it."

"I'm Marlo Thomas's friend," I joked with myself as I hung up the phone, but I loved how Grandma's words even spoke to the heart of *That Girl*.

"Happiness, you make them." Grandma's words have played like a mantra in my mind, but I wasn't quite sure how it applied in my facing-forty-and-childless crisis. What's the next best thing to making yourself happy? Trying to bring happiness to someone else, right?

So that's when I planned an impromptu trip to Pelican Bay.

———

Even though I wake up early after a night spent in the Crescent City Travelodge, the prison waiting room is already packed when I arrive at 8:45. The CO at the desk hands the woman in front of me a pass to be filled out and asks, "GP or SHU?" He gets distracted before he can hear her ask back, "What's GP?" So I explain, "General Population," and add with a laugh, "Yes, my mother is so proud that I can so readily answer a question like that." And we share a nervous laugh.

Sitting in the waiting area is a little like being at Motor Vehicles and I am joined by a potpourri of people thrust into this sterile setting. As the corrections officers process visitors through the metal detectors, seats become vacant, and I sit down on a plastic-cushioned bench against the right wall between the water fountain and the vending machines. I notice that a woman sitting on a similar bench across from me in the middle of the room is wearing the same black-and-white sweater I recently bought specifically for prison wear.

"Nice top," I say when she looks my way. "I see you decided to wear a T-shirt under as well." Our black sweaters feature a white collar and cuffs, and we both opted to wear a black "tee" underneath in case the V-necks are deemed too low-cut for the prison dress code.

"Why risk having to change?" she says. She's blond and wears her hair in a short curled style that looks like she has it set regularly at a beauty salon. She's probably in her late fifties or early sixties, and I assume she is visiting her son. She is with a younger woman who is also modestly dressed, but I cannot say the same for all of the women in the room. At the counter the guard sends an attractive Hispanic woman back to her car to change and tells her she needs to wear something that covers the tattoo on her chest completely. I have never seen a woman with someone's name tattooed on her chest before, but I try not to be judgmental. They are wives, girlfriends, and mothers. High heels are popular with the younger women. Every exposed toenail in the place is polished—even mine.

In an early correspondence Rory wrote how he missed just about every little thing about women—especially "pretty girls in summer dresses with painted toe nails." I wasn't about to go so far as to give him the summer dress fantasy, but I figure I could at least give him a look at my painted toenails. My sweater is a little boxy and I am wearing black-and-white checkered capri pants. I think about how all the women in this room must have spent the morning in careful wardrobe-selection mode, wanting to please an inmate but not get the guard's attention. A white woman with long, straight brown hair who looks about thirty catches my eye because she looks so old-fashionedly feminine in her fifties vintage skirt. I notice two roses tattooed on the back of her calves when she gets up to go to the ladies' room.

Those going to Security Housing Unit (SHU) to visit are processed first, because they have to take a bus inside the prison compound to get to the supermax part of the facility on the other side of GP's housing units and yards. Their visits are always behind glass and have to be made by appointment. GP visitors with an approved visitor's form on file do not need appointments.

I sit and mind my own business until my name is called. The guard pronounces the *ll*'s in Kinsella like a *y*, the Hispanic way. As I am processed through I realize that while it may not be a totally comfortable experience going through the gated pens and past the razor wire and electric death fences, this time it's much less unsettling. Still, I frown as I notice that Officer Buck Tooth is at the front desk inside the visiting room again. I try to be cordial to the guard as he assigns me a table, the same one I had last time, although I doubt he remembers. It takes about a half hour, but when Rory comes out he looks right at me, cocks his head back, and drops his jaw as he walks over to Buck Tooth to hand him his ID.

We're both smiling as I stand up to share a great big hug.

"You surprised?" I ask.

"Hell, yeah," he says, with a little hickish drawl that comes out from time to time in his speech. "I mean, when they popped my door and said I had a visitor I was hoping, but . . . I thought it might be my mom."

He smiles a crooked smile at me as he sits down with his back to the guard. That smile makes me think he's glad it's me and not his mom for this visit.

He says my hands are cold when he takes them into his and immediately inspects my shredded cuticles. On our first visit in June Rory loved the revelation that we shared the nervous habit of picking at our cuticles, especially on our thumbs. He likes to find these little things we have in common.

Freedom is something we don't have in common. The prison got locked down for about a month after my June visit when one inmate stabbed another. Then when Rory finally got access to a phone and called my number, the collect call was denied. He didn't know it, but I had changed my phone carrier and I didn't realize that the new company didn't accept collect calls. When he received my answer to his giddy-in-love letter saying our friendship had to be platonic and when he couldn't get me on the phone, he thought he had really screwed things up. We laugh about it now, but it had taken several weeks for us to get things cleared up.

I had gotten used to Rory calling me on Sunday nights, and when I didn't hear from him, I worried. I also rented the first season of the HBO show *Oz*, which is basically a nighttime soap opera set in a maximum-security prison. When I tell Rory about this I can see he is pleased that I missed him.

"Don't tell me, there was a shower scene," he says about *Oz*, rolling his eyes. "There's always a shower scene in every movie about prison."

When the public thinks of prison, it thinks of rape. So I ask him about it.

"Sure, there are guys having sex. But in the whole time I've been here, I've never heard of a rape."

"Did you ever have any trouble with someone interested in you like that?"

While Rory was in jail awaiting sentencing the prosecuters talked about the death penalty as a real possibility. He fell into a depression and used the money his mother sent him to buy food from the canteen. "I was *huge* when I got here," he says. "So nobody wanted me—the predators, the gangs, they left me alone. I barely fit into the largest-size prison blues they had. And the first time I was out in the yard they stripped us down. That was just what I needed: to be fat and naked on my first day."

It took him over two years, but he dropped 172 pounds. "At first I couldn't even do real push-ups; I had to start with girly push-ups. Real macho, huh?"

"So it was your weight that saved you from something that might have happened?"

"Yeah, after two years I wasn't a fish anymore, so nobody could do anything."

I ask him who his friends are.

"Well, *yoooou*," he says, widening his eyes and smiling his crooked smile.

"Come on, I mean in there."

Rory's had the same celly for the last five of his eight years at Pelican Bay. "He's like my brother," he says of Tony. "He's back-East mafia and when I first met him I couldn't stand him. He was always trying to push that mafia thing in your face."

Rory lapses into an anecdote about how one time he and Tony were showering on the tier and the cop let out two black dudes who were about to attack a skinny white kid. "We jumped 'em, *buck naked,*" he says proudly, with an emphasis on the last two words that I know is for my benefit. "The cop came at us with his pepper spray but we just kept at 'em. That one was talked about for a long time in here."

The black dudes were sent to the hole, and Rory and Tony got to finish their showers before going back to their cell.

"Why didn't they do anything to you?" I ask.

"That cop risked my life by letting those guys out like that, and he knew it," says Rory, narrowing his gaze. "That guy's gotta walk around every day in here, too, and me and Tony never did anything to him." The power play between the guards and the inmates is a delicate business, I think, although I am not so sure "delicate" is the appropriate word, given the setting. "You just gotta let them know that you know who you are—and you know who they are," Rory explains. "A guy who's just getting on you, to get on you, isn't gonna get any respect. Honestly, if they all just left me alone in my cell, I'd be perfectly happy."

"What would make me happy right now is a cup of coffee," I say. As we walk over to the vending machines I talk about how I am such a creature of habit. Every morning I set up the coffee machine at home the night before. Then when my alarm goes off I press the snooze, get out of bed, and go into the kitchen and push the button on the coffeemaker. Then I take a banana and go back to bed and wait for the coffee to brew.

He smiles up at me from where he is crouched before the machine to retrieve my coffee and says, "I like the idea of you all cuddly and cute, in bed with your banana."

"Oh, stop," I say, nudging him as he stands up.

He is still smiling when we get back to our table. "Come on, it's just too adorable, you and your banana."

"Okay, well . . . let's just change the subject. If Tony was such a jerk, why did you want to live with him?"

My question makes Rory laugh at himself. "I like challenges," he answers. "Living with a guy 24/7 in a toilet, it's hard to keep up the bravado." Rory calls Tony on his stuff, like his claim to be all Buddhist, Taoist now. "He's still a raging Italian."

"Hey," I mock-protest, "I'm Italian."

Bottom line, Tony makes Rory laugh and he enjoys picking at Tony's tough guy identity. "People in here try to give themselves labels," says Rory. "Like that guy over there, he's not so sure what or who he is yet."

I turn to look at a man sitting across from the woman with the tattooed roses on her calves. He's at least six foot three, 230 pounds maybe, with a shaved head and tattoos sprouting from every visible opening in his clothing. One looks like a vine and snakes up his neck and stops at the base of his shaved skull.

"He doesn't know if he's a skinhead or what, but they are not going to give him long to sit on that fence," says Rory, shaking his head back and forth a little to gently snap a kink in his neck. He sighs and smiles after the snap.

"What'd he do?" I ask. While it is not really polite to inquire about someone's crimes to their family, I imagine, like me, the visitors ask the inmate they are visiting about other men's crimes.

"I don't know; he got transferred here, some kind of hate-crime thing." Rory sits back and stretches out his interlocked hands, and I wonder if he thinks he impresses me with this stuff. I am not so much impressed as intrigued.

"How do you deal with it, the fear?" I ask.

"I remember when I first got here thinking that I know I am not the monster they say that I am," he continues, leaning in on the table so that no one else can hear, "but these guys really are." I get a faint whiff of tobacco and soap as I size Rory up—part bravado, part vulnerability, all self-satisfaction without arrogance. He's cute and cocky at the same time.

I suspect that the incident in which Tony and Rory saved the white kid from the black inmates didn't exactly go down as he played it out for me, and I remember how my defense attorney friend had told me that cons are master manipulators. It really doesn't matter. We all choose the way we show ourselves to others, don't we?

One way I choose to show Rory who I am is through pictures.

"It's a beautiful day, let's go sit outside," I suggest.

After he sits down next to me at one of those cement picnic tables, he asks me, "Are you okay?"

"No," I answer honestly. "I haven't been okay all summer. It's amazing how you can walk around and people don't even notice there is anything wrong." I paused to collect my thoughts. "I had lunch the other day with a publisher, an older guy who I know is enamored of me. He's married, so it's nothing like that, but he told me how delightful it was to watch me navigate the world, with my energy and sparkle."

Despite appearances, I hadn't felt at all *That Girl*–ish all summer. "All I can do when I get back to my lonely little apartment is think that I just want to get over this kid thing once and for all," I tell Rory, although he has already made it clear that he thinks I don't need a man to have a kid. I joke with Rory that between knowing him and a radical environmentalist friend, I suspect my phone is tapped.

"I can just see the guys switching shifts to listen in on my phone calls when one says to the other, 'I wish she'd just turn forty already and get it over with!' " which makes us both laugh. "C'mon, what guy is going to want to get involved with me with all of that hanging over my head? It's just better I deal with it." I haven't actually tried online dating but I browse occasionally, and I tell him that I understand why most of the guys my age on match.com want to meet younger women. "Who wants all that baggage?"

Rory replies that I should be with a younger guy, anyway, and gives me that crooked smile, all pleased with his thirty-year-old self as he nudges my shoulder. I tell him to stop it and move on to the second installment of the "Bridget Kinsella Picture Show." If my mother served as anchor of the pictures last time, this time it's my father.

I start with my dad's picture from the air force taken during the Korean War, where he served in Iceland before he even met my mother. "There's no denying whose daughter I am," I say. Dad looks a little cocky and he squints those crystal blue eyes I inherited from him. "He closed his mouth because he hated his crooked teeth," I tell Rory. "I inherited them from my dad as well."

"You have a beautiful smile," Rory says without missing a beat.

"Braces," I say, noticing that Rory's teeth are not perfect but definitely well placed.

The next picture shows my dad as a young father kneeling in the living room, his baseball jacket thrown on one of the two love seats that were my parents' first pieces of furniture. He's changing my sister Cindy's diaper on a satin comforter that was a baby shower gift. My father practically rebuilt that little bungalow that was my parents' first home, even going so far as to lay down parquet floors. I talk about how my father had this signature whistle, two perfect notes he'd let out as he walked in the back door. "It's a happy man who does that," I observe, "that 'Daddy's home' whistle. I wish I could do it for you now, but I can't whistle."

Dad whistled even in the lean years after he sold the lawn mower shop and struggled for a while trying to find work to support the family. My mother went to work then and we got by, but I knew times were not always easy. There was double-digit inflation and the energy crisis that made even President Carter put on a sweater. But in those days I think you could be poor and not even know it. We'd watch *The Brady Bunch*, and even if our dads weren't clever architects who could design fancy houses and employ housekeepers, we didn't think we were much different from that idealized TV family. Our wardrobe sure was the same.

My brother Patrick took the next picture I show Rory. I think a happy childhood makes it easier to be nostalgic about your family. I tell Rory how my nostalgic view of my relationship with Patrick, three years my senior with my sister Claire between us in age, is akin to that of Scout and Jem from *To Kill a Mockingbird*. Patrick didn't want me becoming too girly (as Claire had so audaciously started to do), and he was always coming up with odd and often tomboyish things for me to try. When playing hide-and-seek in the basement on a rainy day with neighbors, I can remember him talking me into hiding between the wall and the pipes, and if I complained about the dust and spiders then he wasn't going to help me win anymore. He never actually said the words, but they would've sounded right coming from him: "I swear, B, you act more like a girl every day!"

In the photo I am about nine and my hair is in disheveled braids. I sit on top of my mother with my arms held out and curled up. All you can see of her are her arms held slightly higher as we are pretending to be a multiarmed Hindu deity. As with every photo I show Rory he takes in every detail. Claire sits on the other end of the sofa eyeing Patrick warily. It doesn't look like she knows she's in the shot. Rory reads the body language in the image. He thinks Claire is purposefully aloof; I think it's more like I'm the baby and she is used to my grabbing the attention all the time. Yet I can't help but be moved by the obvious physical intimacy between me and my mother—my body unconsciously on top of hers as we goof around.

Above us hang three shelves, but only two appear in the shot—the first holds a complete set of the *World Book Encyclopedia* and on the second some books and issues of *National Geographic*. Above Claire, our framed student portraits ascend the wall: Cindy's a high school freshman, Joey's in his eighthgrade cap and gown, which means Patrick's in sixth, Claire's in fifth, and I'm in third grade. "Third grade, Mrs. Catellano," I remember. It was the only time I was afraid to come home from grammar school with a report card. I had gotten a C in penmanship. This makes Rory laugh because he says he always gets a kick when he sees that sloppy writing on the envelopes of my letters.

"Kinsellas don't get C's," I say. I had gotten myself all worked up about the grade and when my mother saw it—and more important how upset I was over it—she said, "it's only handwriting." Her antidote was a cold glass of Nestlé's Quik.

"I think you are a throwback to a different era," says Rory, and I think he's right.

I try to progress further along in time with the photos. "Here's one of the best pictures I think I have ever taken in my life," I tell Rory. It was the Christmas after Alexei and I bought our own little house on Main Street. It's taken in my parents' condo on the beach. I pose with my first niece and nephew (my sister Cindy's kids) on my lap—four-year-old Melissa's wearing the dress she wore in my brother Joseph's wedding that summer and two-year-old Thomas is squirming in his seasonal sweater/turtleneck/slacks ensemble. At the time I had no reason to believe that I wouldn't be playing out my own version of happy little family.

Skip ahead two Christmases and here's a shot Alexei took of me with my cousin Renea's baby Isabella. The natural lighting in the bedroom puts me in silhouette and Bella gazes up at me adoringly from a sunbeam. He took several shots of us together like this. "I just don't get it," I tell Rory and start to cry. "That was the last Christmas we were together and he took all of these pictures of me posed in a motherhood I would never have. Why would God give this all to me and then take it away?"

Tears fill Rory's eyes and it is as if he entered my body and joined me in my pain. "I'm just so tired of being brave," I say, and the rawness of my wounds coaxes Rory's tears down his face.

He caresses the only part of me he can touch and plays with the hairs coming out of a mole on my forearm. He waits to speak. "You are showing me these for a reason," he says. "Give them to me; give me all of this pain."

We just sit together like that, holding hands, absorbing the sunshine, listening to each other breathe.

"I've cried more since I've known you than I have in my whole life!" he says softly, breaking the spell only slightly.

"You know, when I was driving up here I was thinking that I might let you kiss me," I say. "I know it's not too smart, but I figured I hadn't been kissed in a long time, what the heck, huh?" I shake my head, blow air out of my nostrils—God help me, I'm thinking, but I have to be honest with Rory—and I say, "I just didn't know how much I would want you to kiss me."

"Yeah?" There's that crooked smile again.

I immediately feel the need to explain some ground rules. "This is not an invitation to anything more than it can be, Rory," I tell him. If I sound stilted it is because I am not sure this is a wise idea for me to cross that line, and yet I had decided to cross it, hadn't I? Even on the drive up here. "I cannot fall for you," I tell him. "You would be another unavailable man, and I've had enough of those. You know this."

He keeps caressing those little hairs on my arm and looks right into my eyes when he finally speaks. "I just want to help you to get better and get back out there, finally let go of all the pain. I really mean that. To want anything else, I would have to be really selfish." He looks at me earnestly but then cracks a smile, biting on the tip of his tongue. "I'm just happy I get to kiss you."

"Yeah, well, I wasn't too sure about that and I sure wasn't going to tell you sooner in the visit because you'd get all cocky," I say, and maybe it's the conspiracy or the secrecy of it—who's going to know besides us?—but I start feeling lighter for the first time in months. There's still more than an hour to go until the end of the visit when we can kiss. "Let's go make some popcorn," I suggest.

Before I leave Rory asks his friend Pete to take a couple of

Polaroids of us together, first outside sitting at our table. I look a little shell-shocked but Rory is completely at ease, cocky as I called it, with his arm around my back grabbing my right shoulder and holding my left hand in his in his lap. We take the second picture inside and it nearly gets us in trouble. Rory stands behind me with his arms wrapped around me and my hands are reaching up to his. Buck Tooth comes running at us just as Pete snaps the picture, so I look a little deer-caught-in-headlights, but Rory beams like a man snatching up the woman he holds dear.

"What?" Rory snaps at Buck Tooth.

"You can't stand like that," says the guard.

"What, I can't hug my girl now?"

I take the picture from Pete and go back to the table. Rory and Buck Tooth exchange a few words, but I can't hear what they say—and I don't really want to, anyway.

"He's a jerk," Rory says when he gets back to the table. "He thought I was doing something with my hands. He's got nothing better to do."

As I look at Rory admiring our photo and grinning I wonder how anyone can be that happy with himself surrounded by oppressive guards and violent inmates all the time. But Rory is oblivious—no way Buck Tooth or anyone else is taking away his moment of happiness.

I try not to think of Buck Tooth and where I am when the visit ends and Rory and I get to have our first kiss—but I didn't need to worry about my thoughts, because with the right kiss the world can disappear.

At the end of the visit we stand and it is as if we glide into each other. I put my hands on his shoulders and he puts his on my hips. At the very first touch of our lips the word "awkward" ceased to exist. Our tongues touch lightly and proceed with a dance they had never known before but were born to do. As his breath tumbles into my mouth I forget where we are and let my body ease into the most perfect first kiss. Tender and yearning. His hands now on the small of my back feel as if they were molded to be there. A sense of security washes over me and lingers in the moments after we stop and look at each other, saying nothing.

Wow, is all that comes to mind as I make my way out of the room with the other visitors. I look back to wave and Rory stands at our table and places his hand on his lips. I do the same. Wow, and what have I just done?

On the long ride back I let my jumbled thoughts of the day lead me home. I don't turn the radio on at all until I get stuck in traffic caused by overnight construction on the Richmond Bridge. The last exit before I make my way across the Bay is for San Quentin. I listen to the sound track from the movie *Ragtime*, which was produced by Randy Newman. I listen to an instrumental number over and over again; it's a waltz that makes me dream of dancing with Rory outside below the stars to the sound of a carousel on some mystical boardwalk. Hurricanes and earthquakes.

He's imploring me to hand over all of the pain I am carrying and all the feelings of loss that are flooding over me as I try to come to terms with where I have been and where I might go in my life at forty. He literally wants me to lock all the things holding me back away with him. But is it fair to him? He might be the one to help me finally salvage the damage from my long hurricane, but will he be able to handle the jolt of the earthquake hovering below these beautiful, budding feelings between us when I have to let go? Can I really be that selfish?

All I know is that I haven't felt this heard and understood and cared for by anyone in years. He sees me drowning. Why do I let him see me drowning when with everyone else I fight so hard to appear to be staying afloat? I decide to just let myself feel the blessings of the day and leave it at that.

And I listen to the boardwalk waltz again and again until I am home.

CHAPTER 5

NANCY

I can't watch movies and stuff about prison because when I watched *American History X,* I was totally bummed because I have this total fear that he's going to turn homo on me." It's practically the first thing Nancy says as we get into her mini-SUV and I turn on my tape recorder. I take no offense at Nancy's remark because she has no idea about my history and we had been talking about *Oz* and how odd it is that some of us in the prison auxiliary can get sucked into HBO's maximum-security soap opera.

"Look, I have nothing against gay people, or anyone, really," Nancy says. "I used to even hang out with a couple of drag queens, but I stopped, because when I told them about Sean they teased me all the time that he was going to go gay in prison."

"Sean doesn't seem the type," I offer, which makes her laugh because she is the woman with the tattoos on her calves and her husband is the six-foot-three skinhead with tattoos snaking out of his shirt collar. I make a mental note that she referenced *American History X,* a movie starring Edward Norton as a violent skinhead who goes to prison, gets raped, and does not "go gay" but winds up owing his life to the protection of a black inmate he works with in the laundry. Rory had told me that Sean committed a hate crime, but I don't want to interrupt Nancy's train of thought with an inquiry, and so I wait to ask her about what got Sean sent to Pelican Bay.

"Yeah, it's my total fear," Nancy continues, "so I am always asking Sean about prison sex. And he's like, 'It's not like in the movies, so quit watching that crap.' "

"How long's he been there?" I ask.

"Two and a half years," she says, after a pause. "Why, what's Rory told you?"

I am wondering if she means what Rory might have told me about Sean or about prison sex, but I don't get the chance to ask, because Nancy asks me where I want to go and hang out for a while before we have dinner. I suggest we go to the beach. This time I flew up to Crescent City, tacking it on to a business trip to Seattle to cover a librarians' conference, with my editor's blessing. While I was sitting at the San Francisco airport in the separate gate area United uses for its short shuttle flights, the woman sitting next to me struck up an innocent conversation. She was headed north for a high school reunion and when I told her why I was going up there she did a double take and said, "You don't look like someone who'd have a friend in prison." Her comment made me think of Nancy immediately, because we had talked a few times, and it was my goal this time to get her story. What did it mean to look like someone who'd have a friend in prison?

That morning, as we were waiting to be processed and sent through the metal detectors, I told Nancy about the woman in the airport. "You know," I said, "if she had been looking at you she might have said the same thing, unless, of course, she looked at your tattoos and made some sort of judgment about them. People have stereotypes and that is one reason I want to write about this." And I took a good look at Nancy. She's petite, like me, fair-skinned, too. She's thirty-five but looks much younger. She dresses hip, with a preference for vintage clothing. She wears her straight brown hair long, a couple of inches from her shoulders. Soft bangs frame her face, drawing the eye to her pointed features and beautifully made-up, almond-shaped brown eyes. Her skill with makeup reminds me a little of my neighbor Amber back in Chicago, an actress who never went out of the house without putting her face on, even though she was beautiful without it. Nancy is like that, pretty without makeup, I imagine, and yet more comfortable moving about in the world all put together. I bet she'd wear makeup even while playing softball.

Now, after a day of visiting prison, we are both still dressed in that modest but feminine way that gets us past the guards and still pleases the guys. Come to think of it, we look a little like librarians. Well, now who's making stereotypes, Bridge?

Even though we had never actually hung out together before, Nancy easily took to calling me Bridge without invitation. I do not mind her taking the liberty of using the name usually reserved for talking to myself or preferred by some family and old friends.

"You know, Bridge, I never come out here," Nancy says as she pulls her SUV off the coastal road and into a scenic overview above the beach. "It's a pretty trippy place. There's this weird oppressive thing hanging over the town and it even manifests itself in the ocean, too. When you are driving by it just looks really angry—and that's not how it is down south." Nancy owns a condo in Orange County, but one of the women from the prison lets her stay up here with her for free, which is a big help because Nancy is looking for work and she isn't sure what she wants to do.

Ever since I was a kid growing up at the Jersey shore I have always thought that oceans had this magic way of reflecting my own moods. When I arrived the day before, I'd asked the cab-driver to take this route along the beach on the way to the motel. He was a chatty fellow and told me this was whale-migration season. It was a crisp, clear day and I thought the ocean seemed excited along with me as I continued on this dual path of dis-covering what visiting a man in prison did for other women and uncovering my own truth about my relationship with Rory. No sooner did I have this thought when I spotted a whale's tail flip-ping out of the water. I squealed and the cabbie couldn't believe my luck. But I kept this little bit of wonder to myself, not want-ing to influence Nancy as she tells me her story.

If the ocean seems angry to her in this place, then maybe she is angry, too.

Since Sean's been in Pelican Bay she has made the trip up about five times. All I know so far is that Sean was transferred to Pelican Bay from another prison and is supposed to be trans-ferred somewhere else soon. Nancy has put everything in her life on hold waiting for the transfer. She lives on a home equity line of credit and is getting deeper and deeper into debt.

When we start driving again, I ask her how long she has known Sean. "Ten years," she says. "He was a friend of my old boyfriend's." She laughs at herself. "It was weird because I always had a crush on him, and he always had a crush on me. But it was one of those things: he was my friend's guy and he was younger, too, and he just seemed like a hoodlum." Sean is twenty-eight.

I ask if she went to college. She took some junior college

classes in Spanish and astronomy. She's a voracious reader, but admittedly not great at school. She stays on subject here, though.

"I just never forgot about him, there was just something," she continues. She even went so far as to take her car to his brother's garage just so she could ask about Sean. "So his brother's like, 'He got locked up, why don't you write him?' I was like, 'Okay.' " Her voice gets a little soft but stays chipper. "I was still living with my ex-boyfriend at the time; even though we were broken up, we were splitting the rent. So I write this letter to Sean, 'Hey, how's it going, blah, blah, blah, blah . . . ,' and I never sent it.

"I was going through a lot at the time, breaking up with my ex, other things," she continues. "But a few months later when I did send the letter I walked down to the mailbox because I didn't want to mail it from my house. And I kept toying with the envelope—putting it in and out. And then I dropped it in and something just went off in my head like, 'Man, you just sealed your fate for life.' "

Fate comes up a lot when I talk to women involved with inmates.

Nancy resisted Sean for a few months. "I told him I didn't want to get involved with a jailbird. 'I think you're hot and I think you're cool, but, un-uh, it's not working that way.' And, you know, of course, it did happen that way."

We arrive at the one Thai restaurant in town. As we walk in, Nancy pauses and says, "It sounds so white trash, you know. 'Oh, I met him in prison.' " She stops and rolls her eyes at herself. "But we did have somewhat of a history. Still, people are just so judgmental, which is why I didn't say anything to anyone."

It's not like I was going around telling everyone about my unique friendship with Rory. He was a secret reserved for just a few select girlfriends. My parents thought my interest in Rory was professional—I was helping him get his work published and I might want to write a book about the women I'd met through the prison. So, I understood Nancy's silence about Sean.

After we sit down, Nancy picks up her narrative again. Both she and Sean grew up in Orange County. "He had a weird situation," she says. "His father was a real racist. He grew up with his father in and out of prison so he kind of glorified the whole thing. And his father was abusive to his mother. He once beat up his mother because she cried during *Roots*." Nancy lowers her voice and adopts a mock kick-ass tone, mimicking the racist father saying, " 'You don't cry over a fucking . . . ,' oh, yeah, he did use the N word."

Sean's parents split up and he, as the youngest son in a family of boys, got shifted back and forth between parents. Eventually he went to live with his grandmother. "So he was alone a lot," says Nancy. "By the time he was eleven or twelve he was getting involved in gang things."

I nod and chime in: "With most of them, you know, I think that's their story. Dad beats Mom, leaves Mom." I pause. "His mother tried, but I think every person who was supposed to take care of Rory neglected or abused him in some way."

"Mm-hmm, mm-hmm," Nancy agrees. "But despite everything—and him winding up here—he is a remarkable, sensitive person. His brothers have real issues with women and he's come out pretty strong. He even says that prison was the best thing to happen to him because he was kind of a bully and a knucklehead. He's learned a lot and instead of turning it into a negative thing—like I would've done—he turned it into something worthwhile."

"I don't know if I agree with what you say about yourself," I say.

"I'd get my ass kicked in prison," she answers without missing a beat.

"You come off as a pretty strong personality. . . ."

"Thank you, but . . . I don't know, I left him twice."

We had not even looked at the menu when the waiter comes to take our order. When the waiter leaves I suggest we start with spring rolls.

"Yeah, I wanna get something that is not going to give me bad breath," says Nancy. "I try not to eat garlic the night before I see Sean, or at least two days before."

"Really? You think garlic can last for two days?" I ask.

"Girl, I am not going to risk it," she says. "I'm really paranoid about my breath." She knows herself well, I think, and laughs very easily at her own expense. On TV the night before I had caught a new show on cable called *The Closer*, starring Kyra Sedgwick as a deputy homicide police chief. The actress seemed so at ease in her body, this hard-edged southern woman holding her own in the man's world that is the LAPD. Looking at Nancy, I observe that she seems to occupy her own persona with a similar ease-among-an-unease. She even has sharp, pretty facial features like Sedgwick.

"I want to be fresh and minty," Nancy continues, using a peppermint-gum-commercial voice, "not old and garlicky."

Nancy already told me that she's been on a self-improvement kick lately, giving up meat and alcohol. So I ask if it is okay if I get chicken.

"Girl, please. Oh, I've got to stop saying 'girl.' It just sounds stupid. That's a bad habit of mine, I say, 'Girl, chica, what's up?' And I gotta cut that out."

Nancy picks up her narrative from dropping the letter in the mailbox. That very same day a letter arrived for her from Sean. Was it fate? He was in county jail awaiting sentencing, originally facing twenty-five to life.

"Can I ask what he was charged with?" I ask.

"They call it a hate crime, attempted murder, blah, blah, blah, blah, blah," she says with a nonchalance that I think reflects a selective ignorance when it comes to Sean's criminal activity. At that moment, a waitress arrives at our table. Nancy and I exchange glances with each other and giggle in an "if she only knew" kind of way.

Nancy goes back and forth deciding what to order. "That's totally me," she says. "Picky and indecisive."

One thing she was certain about was that she was in love with Sean when he wrote to her but she fought "tooth and nail" to turn down his proposals. "You think he's hot, don't you?" she asks me.

I am grateful that Nancy doesn't wait for my answer, because even though I have never spoken with Sean and he has been nothing but gracious to me, those tattoos of his scare me, and I think that even if he has reformed his skinhead ways he's capable of horrible things. But I am visiting a convicted murderer, so who am I to judge? Aren't women attracted to the "changed man" all the time? Or perhaps they wish to be the catalyst for change. There's a line from one of those old *Desk Set* movies in which Spencer Tracy says to Katharine Hepburn, "Why do women always fall in love with one man and then try and make him into someone else?" Rory changed himself from the person who committed murder long before I walked into that prison, but I also know that my affection has and is still playing a large role in his continuing road to discovery and redemption. It's part of the pull and satisfaction I get out of our friendship—but I would never marry Rory for it.

Nancy tells me she agreed to marry Sean even before he was sentenced, when he was looking at twenty-five to life. "I told him I'd do it for the conjugals," she continues. "I just convinced myself, I'll just do it for this shallow purpose. But once it actually happened, I didn't want anybody else."

"But you must have people . . . I mean, you're beautiful, you're stylish, you have a great figure," I say.

"Well, thank you," she says. "These babies cost a couple thousand. . . ." She gestures toward her breasts, which now I realize are enormous for her small frame. "Can you tell my husband I'm stylish?"

"But you could get anyone."

"Bridge, can I turn the tape off for a minute?"

I hate when people do this during interviews, but what can I say? She tells me that I can write anything I want but only after Sean is transferred. There are some things she will tell me that she doesn't even want Rory to know about while Sean is still there. So I keep the tape rolling and give her my word that I will wait until the transfer to write what she shares with me. Last year, when she and Sean were separated, there was this biker dude in the OC who wanted to be with her. Sean doesn't know about this temptation, so if I tell Rory and it gets back to Sean, Nancy will have to deal with something that is old news and not relevant to their life now.

"It's like a henhouse in there," says Nancy, about the prison gossip mill. So then, why Sean, who was sentenced to fifteen years five and a half years ago, and is not up for parole for another three years? For Nancy it's this simple: "My man blows everyone out of the water."

To watch them together, as I had that day, is to see two people who shut out the world save for the other. She looks up at him with trust as she fits into the crook of his arm and they walk around the patio snatching an extra embrace before going back to the sanctioned hand-holding. When she pouts, he tries to make her laugh.

"I pick on him," says Nancy, "and he calls me on my stuff."

Before Nancy fell in love with Sean she never wanted to get married or have children. Now she dreams of having kids when he gets out. He'll run a tattoo shop and she'll homeschool the two kids she wants to have, provided her biological clock allows. And they'll live far, far away from Orange County, where Sean got into trouble.

In a book I'd read titled *Women at the Wall*, the author, Laura Fishman, conducted a study of prison wives in Vermont in the 1980s and observed that all the men dreamt of building their women log cabins. Nancy and Sean's postprison heaven meant leaving the OC for a better life, with Dad and Mom and kids hangin' in the tattoo parlor and homeschooling.

Before meeting Sean, Nancy accepted and expected that she'd live her life alone. "I like dogs better than people, anyways," she says, laughing at herself. "I got issues, but who doesn't?"

Among Nancy's issues is her disconnect with her own parents, who adopted her and her three siblings but only doted on her oldest brother. "They're not bad people, they just had too many children," she says. Nancy was molested by a male family member she'd rather not name, but she assured me it was not anyone in her immediate family. Still, she got out of that house as soon as she could at eighteen. Nancy tells me that part of the reason she never wanted to have children of her own had to do with not wanting to repeat her parents' mistakes. I think it probably had something to do with being molested as well.

Nancy relies on her support from a family of close friends. But she didn't even tell them at first when she agreed to marry Sean six months after they started writing to each other. She filed some legal papers that she and Sean both signed and paid the $350 fee. A few weeks later, on one of the few dates a year the prison allows marriages to take place, they exchanged vows without ceremony.

"You know when our anniversary is?" she asks, putting down a spring roll to look directly at me. I notice the wedding band "Sean" tattooed on her ring finger. "February twenty-ninth." She rests a beat, then adds, "They did that on purpose." I wonder how much of the "us against them" mentality plays into her attraction for Sean.

Even though a chaplain at Pelican Bay told me that any woman who marries an inmate in California gets a form listing all of his offenses, I have noticed that many of the wives I've met do not seem too concerned with, or even cognizant of, their husbands' crimes. Nancy is no exception. She doesn't seem to know what offense got Sean transferred to Pelican Bay. Although he doesn't know the particulars, Rory has explained to me that to get sent there from another prison, Sean must have done something, probably race-related and definitely violent, like sticking another inmate with a homemade weapon.

"When he tries to explain that stuff to me it just boggles the mind—and I don't want to know," says Nancy. "He told me one particular story and it made me cry. He told me he was a misguided kid and he wasn't going to do that stuff again."

As more food arrives at the table, Nancy mentions that she prefers to focus on how the relationship, with all of its obstacles and flaws, has helped make them both better people. "He has his beliefs, but he doesn't push 'em on me," she explains. "His whole thing is that he is just against interracial, which, personally, I don't care about, it's their business, but . . . He once stuck up for a black guy in there. That could've gotten him into a lot of trouble." When Nancy asked Sean why he stuck up for a black inmate, he told her that the guy was accused of something he didn't do, and if Sean didn't say something to the guard the black man could have had five years added to his sentence. Sean thought to say nothing would be wrong. It was just the right thing to do.

"He gets arrested for a hate crime and they put him in this place that breeds hate," she says. "I'm proud of him and it's sad, because I never tell him that. I don't want him getting a big head." Nancy explains that one of her biggest issues with men is that she sabotages her relationships. The five years with Sean is her longest relationship. She knows that she is ridiculously jealous.

"I really think that every man, woman, and child wants to do him. It's totally crazy," she says. "I act like it's high school. I am jealous of him, and I think I try to push him away. It's like I am angry with him for being there—and I knew the situation—but it's still stressful."

So what were the stressors that caused Nancy to walk away? For one, the distance got to be a burden. In the two and a half years since Sean's been at Pelican Bay, Nancy has not been able to visit as often as when he was in a Southern California prison. And they never did get those conjugals, because in California, hate crimers, lifers, and sex offenders are denied family visits, but Nancy said that wasn't a problem. Since they hooked up after Sean had already been incarcerated they have never physically been with each other.

"First of all, you don't miss sex. It's not as hard as people think," explains Nancy. "You get to know each other on such a different level. Your relationship transcends everything, because once you throw the physical stuff into the mix you get stagnant for a while. And that's never happened to us." Part of her thinks it almost serves her right, not getting the conjugals, since she had agreed to marry him originally for such a shallow reason. "Now, what does that say about me and my thoughts on marriage?" she asks. "But once I got into it, I took it very seriously."

Since I am not supposed to talk with Sean in the visiting room, much less interview him, I cannot know how Sean feels about the stresses of his sexless marriage.

Nancy says that the biggest issue for them was how she made her living.

"I'm an open book," she tells me, "but there are certain things I can't tell you until he gets transferred, then I'll tell you everything." Apparently, Sean is not all that keen about Nancy and me spending time together. While he was locked up in Southern California, Nancy met his celly's girlfriend and the two women started to hang out together. Something she told the celly's girl got misconstrued and it came to blows for Sean and his celly. "So he's like, 'I don't want you hanging out with anybody's wife or girlfriend,' and I told him you were cool and that we hit it off. Still, he doesn't want me blabbing everything."

Her job was an issue but she holds back from telling me what it was, offering only that it was legal, didn't require education, and that she made a lot of money doing it.

She didn't see Sean for eighteen months, but they sent angry letters back and forth. She planned to go up there one last time to end it and get some closure, but then she was pulled back in. "He calls me on my stuff," she repeats herself. "Maybe it sounds childish, but I think we were fated to be together. It's kind of like a test: I am finally getting my jackpot but I am really going to have to work at it with him in there." She says he is everything she ever wanted in a man—she just hates the situation. "He's got the total feminine, sensitive side, and then he's got the total tough-guy thing going on—and I love that."

I ask her if she thinks he is ready to get out.

"Sometimes I think he is. We talked about this today, and he said he thinks he's got it all together and then he'll go off on some guy and know he doesn't have it all together," she says. A few weeks ago, one of the guards got on Sean's case for kissing Nancy's hand and Sean mouthed off at the guy. "Then today when he came out, the cop was in the back when they were stripping out and Sean apologized. He's really trying and really growing up in there."

Even with all his growth, she admits that she doesn't really know what he will be like when he gets out. "He's a little like the *Sleeping with the Enemy* husband," she says, referring to a movie in which Julia Roberts's character's husband has obsessive-compulsive disorder and she fakes her own death to get away from him. It's not a hopeful image. OCD is pretty common among prisoners; some can shake it when they get out, others can't. Nancy doesn't dwell on it too much. "Sean says he folds up his dirty laundry," she says, laughing. "Now there's something wrong with that." Whatever happens, Nancy says she'll take it the only way she can—one day at a time.

When the check arrives and I pay it, she thanks me and gently probes me about how I got involved with Rory. I give her the *Reader's Digest* version: gay ex-husband, never got over it, how I can't even bear to be with my family and watch them all have kids. Then I explain how loving Rory is making me better. And how I know I will crush him when I have to pull away, but that is the whole point. "He says, 'I love you so much I love you without me,' " I tell her.

"Oh, man, Bridge, so you can totally relate to my fear," she says, latching onto the gay ex detail.

"Maybe that's part of my problem, I never suspected Alexei was gay," I say, adding, "but, you know, he did like Bronski Beat," referring to the eighties band in which the lead singer sang in falsetto about a gay boy running away from home. I've learned to punctuate my story with comic relief.

We decide we don't feel like calling it a night just yet, and even though she gave up drinking, Nancy suggests we hit one of the local bars. "Let's see what passes as a nightlife in this town," she says, driving toward a dive bar in Tsunami Landing. I notice a tattoo bracelet on her left arm, a rope-knot design with the word "precious" at the center on the inside of her wrist.

"I guess it's a reminder of what is precious inside you," I say.

"No, it's to remind me that other people are precious," she says, laughing really hard and looking at me sideways. "But I always forget to look at it." That makes us both laugh at how she does things to better herself but doesn't always follow through. She parks the car and says, "I kinda wish I hadn't quit drinking now."

"Oh, we don't have to go to a bar, we can go get some coffee or something," I offer.

"Oh, no, it's not the bar or the booze that is going to tempt me—it's *you*," she says, smirking and crinkling her eyes. "I just wanna hang with you, and I know we could get ourselves into trouble. But I made a promise, and I'm not going to drink."

It's early, just about 6:30, and the bar is pretty empty. It's your typical small-town dive bar. It's long and narrow but there's an opening into a larger side room with tables. The DJ is in the side room spinning tunes for an empty dance floor. We sit at the bar in the narrow room next to a group of rowdy guys.

"Tweakers," Nancy calls the guys, meth users. "Whaddyawant?" Nancy buys the drinks, a vodka tonic for me and a nonalcoholic beer for her.

"Wow, you have a lot to figure out when you get back home," I say. I try to get her to tell me about the job she quit.

"C'mon, didn't you get it?" she asks, gesturing to her augmented breasts. Then it hits me: how does a woman make a lot of money doing something legal that her husband wouldn't like? She was a stripper.

"Dancing was actually pretty cool," she says. "And I'll tell you, I'd rather do it for blue-collar guys than white-collar guys any day. White-collar guys have a sense of entitlement." She tried to tell Sean that she didn't want any of those guys, it was only how she made money.

"It caused us a lot of problems because he's jealous. But you know what, I told him, 'You're not paying my way and I've been doing this long before you were in my life, and it's all I've ever done. I'm not paying eight-hundred dollar phone bills for you to pinch me on this," says Nancy. That's when she walked away for eighteen months and started refusing his collect-only calls. She tells me that when your guy is in prison and you love him and miss him it's really hard to refuse those calls. If no one else is in line for the phone he can call back again and again, racking up the phone bill in the process.

Nancy got fed up with it all, but just seeing Sean again wooed her back.

"I quit that work," she says. "Please, none of the girls know." Again she tells me that once Sean is moved I can write anything. She quit stripping about six months ago with no backup plan. "So I came up here to be with him and I just get more debts."

I had heard from "the girls"—the inmates' women I have gotten to know a little on my prison visits—that Nancy had taken some classes to be a nurse's aid and I ask her how that went.

"I have a lot of respect for people who do that, but basically you're a butt wiper for minimum wage. And with my issues with other people's bodies and stuff, I don't know what I was thinking," she says, laughing at herself again. "I told Sean I just want to be a housewife, that's the perfect job for me. But no one else is going to take care of me. Stuff always seems to work out, but to go from making two grand a week to nothing . . ." Her biggest fear is that she will lose her condo, the only thing she has for her future. Her plan is to move out and rent it, then go stay with the woman who offered her a free place up here until Sean's transfer comes through.

"This is the first time I put someone else first, you know, so that's a big deal for me," she says. "Progress, huh?"

Then she leans into me and says in a voice meant for secrets, "You know, Bridge, I hate men. I can't stand 'em. They're pigs. They're pervs. They're liars."

Somehow it makes bizarre sense for Nancy, with her sexually abused background and her hatred of men, to seek out a job that gives her sexual power over men and a relationship with a man in a place that lets her have most of the control. Still, I worry if Nancy is kidding herself about Sean and that he just might not be the sensitive guy she imagines him to be. But I figure it is not for me to say.

"Why not be a lesbian?" I joke.

"A lot of people will think that's why you're with him," says Nancy. "I was molested and everything—we're a total cliché. C'mon let's go dance. There's this new song they keep playing on the radio and I'll get the DJ to play it."

So, with Nancy holding her implants in place, we bounce around on the empty dance floor dressed in our conservative prison-approved clothes, and Nancy introduces me to the music of the Black Eyed Peas.

The next morning as we wait to be processed into the prison, Nancy tells me she has something she wants to give me after the visit. "It's a sweater I got at a vintage store that Sean tells me makes me look like an old lady, but I like it," she says.

Nancy and I exchange a few extra smiles across the room during the visit, but Sean eyes me suspiciously. The civilians are allowed to take bathroom breaks anytime they want, but the inmates have to wait until an extra guard is on hand to take them one by one into the back room where they get stripped down before being allowed to go to the bathroom. Rory and Sean wind up next to each other in line and I can see them chatting a little.

When Rory gets back to our table he says he tried to approach Sean, saying something friendly about how their girls hung out together last night, and Sean just snapped about how Nancy better not have drunk anything. "I don't know about that guy," says Rory. "I just hope he's okay for *her* sake."

After the visit Nancy gives me a fuzzy pink sweater and a lift back to the Travelodge before heading out to the house where she is staying, which I learn is actually a couple of hours away. It's still better than the drive from Orange County.

I wear the sweater the next day and take a taxi out to the dinky airport, asking the woman cabdriver to go by the beach. I tell her that I saw a whale when I came in on Friday. "That was you?" she says. Apparently my excited reaction to my first whale sighting struck the first cabdriver enough that he mentioned it to this woman. That's how small this town can be.

About six months later, while I am in Crescent City again, I get a call on my cell from Nancy as I was about to walk into Wal-Mart as a way to pass some time between my Saturday and Sunday visits.

"Well, I don't want to interrupt your Wal-Mart shopping," she jokes. I had heard that Sean was transferred several months ago to a prison closer to Nancy's home in Orange County, but that she still had to drive a few hours to visit him. I was hoping she had good news.

"How's it going with you guys?" I ask.

"Girl, he was totally cheating on me," she says. I couldn't believe it. How do you cheat from prison? After the transfer, Sean wrote to his ex-girlfriend and told her she could visit when his wife wasn't there. I guess that would do it. One of the other women visitors told Nancy about it.

"I'm sorry, Nancy."

"I was really pissed, but it's totally for the best," she answers. Nancy got a job waitressing and is looking into taking classes at a community college again. She's done with prisoners and done with stripping, even though she still has to dig herself out of a mountain of debt she amassed trying to be with Sean. Instead of being bitter, she filed for divorce and got on with her life.

"My therapist told me this wasn't a real marriage, and she was right," Nancy says in a remarkably chipper voice. But then she lowers her tone and adds, "You know, Bridge, I worry about you."

"Don't. I'm not going to go there. Promise."

By that time, of course, I had already been there and back again.

CHAPTER 6

GETTIN' MY FORTY ON

Inspired by our August visit, Rory sent me a whopping fourteen-page letter. He asked if I had decided before I got there to just give him a perfect day. He called me his angel. He wrote:

> You are <u>everything</u> [underlined six times] I have ever wanted to love.
>
> I wanted to love you before I ever met you, Bridget.
>
> The fact that I got lost along the way, that I did not meet you until now in this impossible situation . . . Well, just for today . . . Please, Bridget, just for today . . . I am going to pretend that everything is just fine, that the world is kind and life has worked out perfectly . . . Just for today can we be lost soulmates finding each other? I know it is silly, but please let me have this one day forever. Just this one day with you sealed inside my heart forever.
>
> Okay? I know better. I'm all-right with that. Because I am going to heal you, pretty girl. And you will fly away someday, finding the joy and happiness you need out there.

And I will be so incredibly happy for you. But not today. Not this day.

Today you are sixty. Just for a day. And you continue to be all mine.

I laughed at his saying I was sixty, when I agreed I'd be with him as my backup plan for old age. He apologized for coming on so strong, but he didn't let up either, having given himself permission, just while he finished the letter, to pretend everything was perfect. And so began the dreamworld. The only place Rory and Bridget would ever, could ever exist. Would I let even that happen?

Rory didn't give me much of a chance to resist. A week later another letter arrived. And then another letter. He even sent me his most prized possession: the picture we took with his arms around me that had gotten the guard so fired up on our last visit.

Not sure of what all this could, would, or should mean, I started to talk about it more with my friends—select girlfriends, the ones I knew would not judge me. A few of them had already fallen in love vicariously with Rory through his letters I'd read to them. I had to keep reminding one of them in particular that Rory was not a cute, cuddly puppy, but in fact a convicted murderer who was manipulating my feelings and I knew exactly what he was doing. Oh, I still cherished the attention and practically ran to the mailbox to get those letters, but I was also trying to corral my feelings and keep them out of the realm of the impossible.

Rory's attention provided pure romance with none of the hassles of a relationship. A vacationship. Why not take a trip on the USS *Day Dream*? My friends encouraged me to just go with what I was feeling. Who could get hurt? Rory, but then he asked me to let me break his heart by healing mine. After all, the knight in shining armor never actually gets the queen, just the honor of dying for her.

In his second post-kiss letter that arrived Labor Day weekend, Rory wrote that he was being very careful with us: "I am holding your wounded heart in my hands, doing my best to nurture it, heal it, feeding it pieces of my own heart." He had looked up what our double-nine birthdays (mine October, his April) meant in the *I Ching* and discovered it meant "double heaven." He just loved that. That letter came in a card he made with his drawing of Mickey Mouse professing his love for Minnie on the front.

Even though Rory was thirty now, he had been incarcerated since he was nineteen. In many ways, he was courting me like a teenage boy.

His third letter contained his poetry and more assertions of how just knowing me has made him feel human again, not his prison self. He wrote:

She is my razor blade.
Shining, gleaming, so sharp and sleek
That I do not feel the pain until she is gone.
Blood flowing from my heart whenever she moves away.

I want to caress her scars,
To bind them softly,
To seal them with tiny scraps of pure light,
Take it from her, live with it for her.

Just a boy in love with a razor blade,
Treasuring the wounds I bear for her.

When he called me a razor blade he literally sliced open my core and exposed a truth that even I was unable to name. Instead of wanting to brush my wounds aside or finding them too overwhelming, as others had, Rory craved to carve them into his own flesh.

His words and their intensity soothed and scared me at the same time, mirroring how I felt about our first kiss. It was a good thing I was going to see him again soon.

Every fall I go up to Portland to cover the Pacific Northwest Booksellers Association trade show. This year I rented a car, tucked Rory's poem letter and our picture in my purse, and drove up Interstate 5, stopping at the foot of Mount Shasta. I figured I'd visit Rory on the way back. It's not like I was planning another trip just to see him, I told myself.

Still, Rory filled my thoughts as I drove. Even if I was trying to resist it, I couldn't help how good it felt to be understood so well, so quickly, after so long. Yes, I am a razor blade. I've been a razor blade for years. Where did he come up with that? More importantly, why did it make me feel better?

I knew my emotions were still out of whack. Just a week before I received Rory's poems, I had been an obvious emotional mess during a lunch date with a book editor in San Francisco. My demons still haunted me—the gay ex-husband, the raw pain of being childless with my fortieth birthday fast approaching. Some days they manifested themselves as internal tremors that I couldn't hide. I tried to keep to myself. But I couldn't reschedule lunch again, so I went.

Oh, I looked fine. My hair was in place, my clothes were just so; but this editor had worked with many great spiritual writers, including the Dalai Lama, and she saw right through me. "You're not okay," she leaned into me and said softly. I couldn't lift my sandwich without shaking. I stopped eating. She said she could relate. "Sometimes I just feel like," she said, scrunching her face, "it's just so hard being me."

Instead of feeling mocked, I felt validated. We didn't talk it out; she respected my privacy. But here was this woman, with so many professional accolades to her name, acknowledging that sometimes we all walk around silently screaming for a good hug.

Too bad I found the exact opposite kind of hug up in Portland.

Usually I love the huggy-kissy publishing world—I am part Italian, after all. But there's this one married guy I run into at trade shows who always swoops down on me and hugs me too long and too hard. Every time he sees me he asks me to go have a drink with him or to have lunch. He acts like it's an innocent invitation, but he has also made it clear that he wouldn't mind if we weren't so innocent together. I always find his intentions insulting, and usually I can blow him off. But this time he pushed me.

"C'mon, let's just have a drink. I never get to see you."

There's a reason for that, buddy, I wanted to say, but I don't want to make a big deal out of this. When he didn't take no for an answer, I gave him my cell phone number and decided I'd ignore the call when it came. And he did call, several times.

When I saw him the next morning, he wanted to know what happened. Guess my battery was low, I said. So he pressed again. How about lunch? A drink tonight? I tried to explain that I had to cover an event that evening. He pouted.

It sounds so innocuous, but it really unnerved me.

It is times like this that I hate being single the most. When I was married, even if a guy came on to me, I felt secure because I would never cheat. When you are in love you carry the other person with you everywhere; as a married woman I felt protected whether with my husband or not. This guy's constant pressing made me feel naked.

As it was, I was trying to hold myself together and get through this conference without letting my internal vulnerability and emotional upheaval show. I sure didn't need this guy on top of all of that. I wanted to cry and scream, "Will you just leave me alone!" And really scream it, too, right there on the trade show floor, so that everyone could hear. But I decided to just sidestep again.

That night in my hotel room, I reread my letter from Rory and looked at our picture. The married guy called my cell again, but I didn't answer it. The thought of Rory holding my heart, feeding it pieces of his own, made me feel stronger, less vulnerable.

Of course, when I ran into my insistent pursuer the next day, he pushed me to have a drink with him again. "C'mon, it's the last night," he said. Happily, I told him that I was leaving that afternoon to drive down and visit my friend at Pelican Bay on my way back to the Bay Area. Yeah, buddy, I'd rather spend time with a convicted murderer than hang out with your married-but-would-love-some-hanky-panky sorry butt! I thought.

I couldn't get down to Crescent City fast enough.

Routine is comforting; even the routine of going to prison offers its own brand of comforts. Ironically, I pass the time in my same little Travelodge room watching back-to-back episodes of *Law & Order* the night before going back to visit in prison. I wake up early, walk over to Denny's across the street for breakfast, and the same waitress as on my last visit takes my order and asks me if I am sure I don't want the pancakes that come with my omelet. I dress in black pants, a white long-sleeve T-shirt, and a white scarf with black polka dots.

I drive by the beach on the way to the prison.

Early autumn in northern California is the sunniest time of the year, and it is another bright, sunny morning. Inside the processing room, the Security Housing visitors get processed first. Today it seems to be taking forever. I make small talk with a woman named Liz who is a truck driver.

It's nearly 10:00 a.m. by the time my name is called. This is the latest I've gone into visit and if both Rory and I are not processed through before 10:30, when the prisoner count starts, I might be left sitting in the visiting room alone until it clears at 12:30. Several times a day and at night guards take a physical count of the inmates and no one gets processed in to visit during count.

A female guard with a blond ponytail and bangs that frame her shockingly vivid green eyes tells me I cannot wear my scarf into the prison. I have an idea why scarves are prohibited and guess it might have something to do with possible gang identity. To save me time, the guard suggests I leave the scarf on top of the vending machine next to the metal detector. She wants me to get through before count and I appreciate the gesture. I place the scarf on top of the soda machine next to an Oakland Raiders cap that someone else left behind for safekeeping. I guess hats aren't allowed either. I remind myself that it might be a good idea to pick up a copy of the prison visiting guidelines later, on the way out.

I go through the metal detector without setting it off and through the mechanical gates. To my right along the path stand a series of about five single-story, I'm guessing two-room, bungalow-style buildings where those with such privileges have their conjugal visits. They are connected to each other and each has a penned-in front yard with high walls topped off with barbed wire. The whole structure stands inside a gated fence topped with wire. I want to get a better look, but I also don't want to make myself stand out, and so I only glance at the bungalows.

Rory has told me that even on weekend family visits the inmates are called outside for count. And the phone rings every few hours, just so the guards can keep tabs on them. "They never want you to forget where you are," Rory had said. It doesn't sound very romantic to me.

Rory's over-the-top romantic notions are on my mind as I go into the sterile cafeteria-style visiting room. I am a little nervous because, as much as I have enjoyed Rory's letters and their unabashed expressions of love, I know I have to tell him to tone it down, because I can never let myself fall in love with a lifer.

Rory beams when he comes out and walks over to me with his relaxed, cocky swagger that makes me smile and melt a little inside. We bump noses as we go to kiss hello, and laugh at ourselves. He expected me this time, and he shaved his head and face clean, with the exception of his goatee. He immediately takes my ice-cold hands into his and blows on them to warm them up. He probably will get a talking to from Officer Buck Tooth if he keeps that up, I think. His breath tastes faintly of cigarettes but he smells clean, musky even—Ivory soap laced with fresh earth.

When he resumes looking at me he goes over my face slowly with his eyes, taking in every inch. He has written extensively about how he loves every detail of my face, even the few flaws he will never tell me about, which only make me even more beautiful to him. I look down at our intertwined hands as he takes inventory of my face, assessing my emotional state. Inside, my shaking starts again, but I feel safe in his hands. I make eye contact with him as he brushes my red bangs out of my eyes. The "ice blue eyes" he says are "so deep" he will never find the bottom he craves. All of our communication is transported in our locked gaze. "Here, with me, you are safe now," his eyes tell me.

I tell him that I really liked his razor blade poem and how he managed to leap inside of me and tear out my unspoken truth. Relief washes over me as I say the words out loud. He catches my tears with the nicotine-stained fingers of his right hand. He says he has always been able to see inside of people, and prison has only helped him to better hone that skill. Even on the inside, guys are always letting down their prison facade and telling Rory their secrets.

With me, he says he saw sorrow in my eyes the first time we met, when I dressed like a lawyer and tried not to tell him anything too personal. "It was like you had a big chunk of me inside of you already," he says, "because I know sorrow so well." He wants to be an emotional vampire and soak it all up for me. Sorrow he understands, he says, and he wants to take mine away because he saw in the first minutes we met that it was hurting me.

"You are what love means to me from now on," he tells me. "So why is it that in love, you always give and never take?" He begs me to just take his love and accept its healing powers, so that I can finally move on. He jokes how he wants me to meet this guy-in-my-future whom he calls Phil, who will make all of my dreams come true and give me the family I yearn to have. Even though Rory is a hopeless dreamer, he knows he cannot make this dream come true for me. He also jokes that poor old Phil is going to have to drop dead before I am sixty, because he's not giving up on our plan B. He smiles his crooked smile and says, "That would be just fine with me."

He figured out that if he were held in prison for the longest amount of time that anyone was held in California history, that he'd be eighty-seven when he got out, and that he'd still want me at ninety-seven.

"I'd be dead," I say.

"Oh, live one more day . . . ," he retorts, shaking his head, grinning and biting down on his tongue that sticks out slightly.

"You'd kill me," I say, knowing full well what he'd like to do on that day.

"Yeah, but what a way to go."

I laugh because, even for Rory, this is record time for him to make a sexual comment on our visit. The easy exchange reminds me how well we've gotten to know each other in such a short amount of time.

As we sit together holding hands and I look into his eyes, I know he means what he is saying: he wants me to use him and his love to get better. It is worth it to him just to know real love once. I notice yellow and brown flecks in his blue eyes that make them look like the earth viewed from outer space. My inner shakes seem to subside, although my hands are still cold.

I need more coffee.

Standing near the vending machines I tell him about my encounter with the married guy in Portland and how I hate being that vulnerable. It kills him that he cannot hold me whenever he wants to—but since it is not the beginning or end of the visit, he cannot. Just telling me that he yearns to hold me feels like a hug in that moment.

We go outside and sit next to each other at our favorite cement picnic table and barely speak, locked in a silent exchange that erases the outside world. Safe in this bubble, when I do speak I admit what I never admit: that I am afraid to live fully again, afraid to get what I want, because my experience has been that just when I think I have all I want, I lose it. And I know I won't survive that again. As much as I hate to admit it, it explains why I put up with the guy I was involved with a year before I met Rory who said he loved me but that he never wanted a family. One way to not lose something is to not get it in the first place, and it was a whammy to admit that I had done that myself—choosing to be with someone who would not give me anything. And I let that long-distance relationship claim two years of my life before I wised up.

Until Rory called me a razor blade and made claim to being the one who would bear all of my pain and release me, I had not been honest about my own personal prison I had locked myself in. Why did he get through to me? This murderer?

Eleven years among the fallen, Rory understands the pain of absolute loss. In an early letter Rory had explained that prison is about sorrow for what can never be. The world wouldn't let me express the end of my marriage that way. (C'mon, everyone gets divorced, get over it!) But Rory honors my sorrow—even loves me more for it. In that concrete pen, beneath the razor wire, and looking deeply into his eyes, I finally uncork all of my sorrow and let it pour out. Rory eagerly laps it up and stashes it away inside his heart where he'll never let it hurt me again. When that kind of intense connection happens and you let yourself ride with it, it doesn't matter where you are. It's like being in a spell, literally locked away from the world where only the beating of your hearts matters. Without knowing it, I had been searching for a desert island; I just didn't want to be alone on it.

When we snap out of the spell, Rory says it was as if his heart stopped.

There in the cement nongarden, with all of my pain spilled into Rory, I feel freer and more understood than I have in years. I look up at a lone sparrow sitting on a barbed wire coil, singing.

I tell Rory that I am planning to do something on my big birthday to defang it and embrace it. This makes him very happy, to hear me sound so determined and strong. Strength, I remind him, is what Bridget means in Gaelic. We laugh, because we both know that lately, if anything, I felt like the anti-Bridget. But Rory fell in love with my name before we ever met, and he reminds me that Bridget of Celtic lore was a warrior queen who disarmed her opponents with her beauty. Did he forget to mention that she also supposedly fought naked?

That married man who would not take no for an answer made me feel naked; sitting here with Rory, bantering, I feel swaddled in safety.

One thing I know I want for my birthday is for Rory to write me a special letter to open first thing when I wake up. He says it is a sexy, sexy "thang" to ask.

I hadn't really meant that the letter should be sexual, but of course that's where Rory takes it. The idea scares me only a little bit; I know he's already sexualizing me. And I do wonder how he'd make love to a razor blade on her fortieth birthday, even if only in a letter. Once I agree to let this "pillow letter" be our secret, I am surprised how loved I feel just thinking about it. Rory may have suggested we take this direction, but I am the one who decides to let it happen.

"Just make me safe," I say, looking into his earth eyes.

He takes a moment to brush my hair aside again.

"Always."

I feel a pit in my stomach, a void that only a kiss could fill, but we'll have to wait until the end of the day for that.

———

About an hour and a half before the visit is over, the guard calls
for prisoners with photo ducats to sign up for the camera. Rory
asks his friend Pete to take a picture of us outside. I stand in
front of Rory with his hands on my hips and my hands on top of
his. Pete tells me that Rory hasn't stop talking about me since the
last time I was here. "You should see this guy walkin' around in
there wearin' a goofy grin," Pete says, stretching out the time
Rory and I can pose together. Rory playfully pulls my hips back
into him, which I playfully resist. Pete tilts the camera one way
and then the other, and Rory digs his fingers into my hips.

As the Polaroid develops what comes into focus are two people who've sailed off together into a giddy place of their own
making.

We end the visit with a kiss stoked by the fuel of a secret
passion to be expressed in the pillow letter. With me, never to
be with me, to heal me, only to let me go at the expense of his
heart, Rory agrees to be my secret lover. As we kiss, I can feel his
hands inching south, down from my waist, stopping just at the
top curve of my bottom. "Pillow letter," he says as we separate.
Then I grab the back of his head with both my hands and make
him kiss me again. If this is all the action I can get, then I want
more now!

He really is the best kisser I have ever known.

I blush as I grab my Ziploc bag from the table and take my
place at the end of the line to get out of the visiting room.
Through the glass on the other side I see Rory standing at our
table, holding his right hand over his heart. I bring fingers up to
my lips for just a second. I get my ID from the guard and exit
with the other women.

Pamela, Pete's wife, interrupts but does not break the spell. "Did you have a nice visit?" Pamela's Native American, about my size and age. Her black hair falls in long layers around her face and she smiles broadly.

How can I answer her question, when I think I might be out of my mind for taking this leap with Rory? Yet, I know I want to take this leap. I want this secret love. "Yeah, we always have a good time," I say.

"Pete says that sometimes when we look over at you two it's like you're not even breathing," she says.

"I guess we don't notice anyone else," I offer. Then we make small talk as we walk down the path toward the fences. Pamela waves up at the guard in the tower who is controlling the gates as we walk through them. She lives in town and comes every week to see Pete. Rory introduced me to them on my first visit, and they both have a big smile on their faces whenever they see me here. They just celebrated their eighth wedding anniversary. "That's not going to be mine and Rory's story," I want to blurt out, but decide to congratulate her instead. She wishes me a safe trip back to the Bay Area and I drive again in silence most of the way.

People are going to think I've gone crazy, I tell myself. Yeah, but people also don't need to know everything.

Rory made me feel powerful and safe for the first time in years. And it didn't hurt that he finds me all-out sexier than anyone he has ever known and tells me so every chance he gets.

My girlfriends noticed a change in me immediately when I got back. Shopping after lunch in Berkeley with my friend Serita (the one I always had to remind that Rory is not a puppy), she observed that I seem lighter in spirit than I have ever been in the two years she has known me. Yeah, I am still facing forty but I am not as obsessed with the things I do not have in my life. "You know, your friends are grateful to Rory," she said, going through a rack in the Erica Tanov shop.

That's when I found it, the thing that might help me claim and declaw my fortieth birthday: a very impractical, very expensive, whisper-light, pink cashmere coat. I left the store without buying it, but couldn't stop thinking about it.

That night an older single man with whom I'd had a fun (but never consummated) flirtation over the past few years called me to say he was going to be in San Francisco at the end of October and that he'd like to take me to dinner. I couldn't wait to tell someone, everyone really, about the pink cashmere coat and my determination to face forty with gusto. Rick and I have had some pretty intense talks and I know that part of the reason we never hooked up is that he understands I still have things to work out about my marriage and my life. Oh, and he never wanted kids.

Rick told me "to come on in the water's fine" in the fourth decade of life. Oh, and, by the way, would I show up at his hotel room wearing just the pink cashmere coat? With that little suggestion, I decided I had to buy the coat. Whether I'd show up for my Halloween date with Rick ready to trick or treat, I had no idea, but I liked the idea of it. It's something Rory would suggest.

When Rory called a few days later, he immediately heard the new joy in the lighter timbre of my voice. "What happened?" he asked as soon as I accepted the charges and said hello. I told him about the coat (leaving Rick out of it) and my plan to invite twenty fabulous women I know to don something that makes them feel extraordinary and join me for lunch on my fortieth birthday at a fancy restaurant on the bay in Berkeley, where the pink coat would be unveiled.

I was very proud of myself for having cultivated friendships with twenty strong, powerful, independent women in just the two years that I'd lived in the Bay Area. True, I'd met all of them through my publishing job, but that's not why they were coming to lunch.

All that trepidation I'd felt leading up to the event fell away, and as the big day approached it felt as if the world was celebrating with me. A few days before "B-day" (*B* for birthday, and *B* for Bridget's special day), I got a card from my parents with a $500 check in it. When I called to thank them for the coat check I had never asked for, my ever-practical mom said she only wanted to send me half, "but Daddy insisted."

Rory's pillow letter did not arrive in time for the big day, but I woke up that Thursday morning to the sound of the phone ringing and a mechanical female voice saying, "This is a VSSI collect call from [in his voice] Rory [back to the mechanical voice], an inmate at Pelican Bay State Prison. To accept and pay for the call . . . dial . . . five . . . now." I was in shock to hear those now-familiar words, bright and early on B-day, because Rory usually could call only in the evenings or on weekend mornings.

"Happy birthday, pretty girl!" Rory's was the first voice I heard on my big day.

"Yay!" and "How?" I said. I wanted to know how he got the phone on a Thursday morning.

He said he asked a guard if he might be able to call a special girl on her fortieth birthday and the guard said, "Hey, look, somebody left the phone on from last night. And I just need to go over there for a while . . ."

That's how I got my fortieth birthday wake-up call from my secret lover.

It was the perfect start to a beautiful day. I was showered with flowers—the most beautiful of about a half-dozen bouquets, of course, came from my cousin Carolyn (a former florist) and her husband, Val. But the flowers my sisters sent were not too shabby, either. My New York office sent the biggest bouquet; when I called my editor to thank her, she said she was glad I was happy, but wished it had been her idea to send them. We both knew the bouquet was the handiwork of Dick Donahue, one of the features editors at the magazine.

Everybody I told about my pink-cashmere-coat lunch wanted to come. A few of my guy friends even threatened to crash. On B-day the weather was too warm to wear the coat, but I brought it along and hid it in the back at the restaurant to show later.

The manager of Skates on the Bay arranged for us to have a long table in the middle of the restaurant with a great view of San Francisco Bay and the Golden Gate Bridge. I placed pink bath salts on everyone's place. I wore a pink top and my favorite black pleated skirt and high heels—very classy. I would wait to pull out the coat when everyone had arrived. Yes, I have no problem with being the center of attention, and my friends were more than happy to fawn over me. My friend Erica said it was her birthday, too, although she had already turned forty a couple of years before. She gave me flowers. My friend Jennifer, whose birthday was in a week, the same day as Oscar Wilde's birthday, came dressed as Wilde in a smoking jacket and a gentleman's fancy pants. Kathleen brought me a tiara with "40" on it in silver glitter. At one point I glanced over at my friend Kathi and gushed, "I just love my party!"

Then when I thought I couldn't be even one millimeter more happy than I already was, the girls presented me with a gift certificate for a boutique in Oakland where, shopping with my friend Karen a few days before, I had tried on a fabulous cocktail dress that I just couldn't afford. She'd e-mailed the girls behind my back and got them all to chip in and get the dress for me. I had to admit I felt a little pang of emptiness because, even though Rory had sent me a painting he made for my birthday along with a short story that imagined us together with me as the treasured wife and mother I had always wanted to be, the truth is I was no one's wife or mother. No husband was going to be buying me that special fortieth birthday gift, which saddened me.

Then the girls did this beautiful thing, and Rory's call started the day, and I had my coat and the sadness disappeared.

I wallowed in the effervescence of joy I felt and everyone (and I mean everyone) who came into contact with me that day knew it was my special birthday. The guy at the private mailbox place still says "Happy Birthday" to me whenever I go in there, remembering my beaming face on my fortieth. When I told the Indian guy at the convenience store that it was my fortieth, he said, "Mine too!"

The joy bubbled over the phone and into Rory's ear in prison when he called again that night. It all felt that much more real telling him about it. At first, he was disappointed that his pillow letter hadn't arrived in time, but hearing my happy voice mattered more to him than anything.

The next day I practically ran to my mailbox. My stomach dropped at the sight of a single envelope with his penciled

handwriting on it. It still scared me a little to be taking this intimate leap, so I waited to read the letter before I went to bed that
night. I held my breath and opened it:

> *It is my only secret now, that I like to wake up early
> sometimes to watch you sleep. You are always so radiant in
> the morning, sleeping right next to me yet far away and
> dreaming, breathing so deep and easy.*
>
> *And I am your "required sleeping inches" away, propped
> up on one elbow, staring at your bare face, so still and clear,
> your beauty caught slack in peaceful slumber like a paint-
> ing. The face of an angel, of all that I have ever hoped to
> love in this life. And I can feel the warmth of your delicious
> naked body reaching out to me under the covers. It calls to
> me, this warmth. Beckons me, does your perfect flesh, creat-
> ing a hunger in me so that my mouth waters and my heart
> pounds so loudly that I fear it might wake you.*
>
> *It would ruin my plans for you to wake now.*

He painted a tender portrait of my birthday morning being
awakened by a man I've loved for a lifetime, even if only in a fantasy world. The love expressed in it was real, and it transported
me far away from the damage of my past and the emptiness of
not having my own nuclear family.

Once I tackled the daunting milestone, which was really
more like a millstone, I accepted that fate and the future would
work out. I didn't know where or how I was going to fill the
emptiness that had been suffocating me, but I knew I would
figure it out, because unhappiness was never my nature and
Rory's love reminded me of that.

Rory also reminded me that I could feel safe in being sexy.

Even though he was not the man I drove across the Bay Bridge to meet, giggling as I paid the toll while wearing just my pink coat and high heels for the occasion, Rory's love freed me from the very real fear I had developed of sex. Until I met Rory, I hadn't been able to articulate the pain of not only being rejected by my husband but having him reject my whole gender. You say your ex is gay and people ask, Well, didn't you know? Or they say they know so many people that happened to, which does nothing to make me feel better. Instead of deflecting my deepest wound, Rory seized it and offered a kind of sexual healing that was very different from what Marvin Gaye sang about.

And he did it knowing he'd never physically get to benefit from my newfound sexuality. He wanted me to fly for my sake. Driving over the bridge in my pink coat, I soared.

CHAPTER 7

ANGELS AND DEMONS

rick or Treat."

I sang it as I tossed a mini-bag of M&M's at Rick when he opened his hotel room door on Halloween. I stood in the hallway smirking, wearing nothing but a pink coat about the same shade as my skin. Oh, nothing too risqué transpired; my friend Marissa said I am the only woman she knows who could show up at a guy's hotel room wearing just an overcoat and not have sex with him. But that's not what our flirtation was about. The art of the tease can sometimes be just as fun as the conquest, and we clearly mutually enjoyed this tease. We kissed sweetly, not passionately. He engaged in some PG-rated, strategic touching inside my coat to make sure I was actually naked, as promised. I didn't want to have sex with him. I just wanted to feel sexy.

Besides, I think he knew I still had lots to resolve for myself before I could be involved with anyone. So I slipped into the bathroom and into the cocktail dress the girls had bought for me. He helped me on with my coat and I took his arm as we walked out of the hotel. He was a perfect gentleman (aside from having suggested I show up at his room wearing just a cashmere coat), and it suited me perfectly.

Since it was Halloween and everyone in San Francisco goes to watch the parade in the Castro, we had the restaurant to ourselves when we got there. The waiter told us that it was possible to order half-size portions of both entrées and wine as a way to sample more of the menu, which we discussed in great detail. Then, when it came time to order, Rick did the most romantic thing: he ordered for me, based on my stated preferences for food and grape.

After my date with Rick I opened myself up to the idea of dating again. As the fall progressed, I truly was beginning to let go of the past. Rory held my razor blade self, releasing me from it. Or so I thought.

In November, while attending a literary event at a local bookstore, I met an alarmingly charming psychologist who charmed me even more when he said I reminded him of the redhead on *Sex and the City*. The bookseller saw us talking all night and she pulled me aside at one point to assure me he was a really great guy. "One of my favorite customers," I think were her exact words. So when he asked me out I said, "Sure."

I saw it as progress on my part. I had lightened up. It didn't even bother me when I told my sister and her husband about the upcoming date with the shrink and she said, "Oh, no, Bridge, I don't know if that's such a good idea" (because I already think too much for my own good), and he said, "That sounds like a good match to me." It was just a date, and at least I was getting out there.

He picked me up at my apartment and we went to the majestic Claremont Hotel in Berkeley for a drink. Steve had just come from a family wedding and so I got dressed up to match his attire. The seating at the lounge was such that we wound up sharing our table with other people. The first couple we sat with thought Steve and I were married, because they said we looked so good together. Steve was about six feet tall, slender, but not skinny. His hair was just starting to go salt-and-pepper.

I was attracted to him; it was just too bad he had ants in his pants. Steve kept getting up to check on the football game on TV at the bar or to pop in on the holiday party that was in progress down the hall. He'd brush my leg or make some kind of intimate but not too pushy gesture, before he'd get up or sit down so I didn't feel completely ignored or undesirable. Finally, I asked if he was ever planning on just talking with me, his date, and not popping up and down.

Then he asked me the question he said he asks all the women he dates: "Were you sexually abused as a child?" My face must have gone ashen and I didn't know what to say. He took my reaction to mean that I had been abused. He explained that his ex-wife had been abused, and it caused the end of his marriage. I told him I could relate and that at least he had kids and his wife didn't discover she was gay like my ex did. I got upset. The tears couldn't be stopped. Part of it was the shock of the question. And I hated that my story hinged on sexual abuse, even if I hadn't been the one abused.

Steve's question threw me for more than a loop. Who asks something like that—and on a first date? I knew right then and there that there would be no second date. Did I want another martini? He'd already drunk too much to drive and had gotten a room for himself at the hotel and was going to send me home in a cab, so why not have another drink? Of course, I was more than welcomed to stay with him.

If that was dating, who needed it? And it happened just days before Thanksgiving, the holiday eight years ago on which my ex-husband chose to tell me he just couldn't be married to anyone, without any more of an explanation. I could feel the razor's edge cutting into me again. I spent Thanksgiving Day with friends but then I had that whole long weekend to fill.

Time to escape again.

This time, Officer Buck Tooth is behind the counter in the processing center. I walk up to the desk with a confident step, because Buck Tooth had watched Rory and me very closely on our last two visits and he wrote Rory up after the last kiss we shared. Rory sent me a copy of the report because he thought I'd get a kick out of it. Citing the date and time of the "incident," the report read: "While working as A-Visiting Officer, I observed Inmate MEHAN, K-78728, placed both of his hands on his visitor's butt and rubbed up and down while kissing excessively. MEHAN then stopped and briefly talked with his visitor again before engaging in another excessive kiss. Following that kiss MEHAN looked around and then finished his visit up with a final excessive kiss. MEHAN shows blatant disregard for the Visiting Rules and the Officers enforcing those rules."

What stood out to me most in the report, aside from the fact that I know well and good that Rory restrained himself when we kissed and certainly did not rub my butt, is how the words "Inmate," "MEHAN," "Visiting Officer," and "Visiting Rules" all commanded capitalization, but that "visitor" did not. I am not sure if this is prison protocol for reports or this officer's own determination, but it reflects how the visitors of inmates are regarded as nonpersons.

I wonder what kind of toll that attitude takes on people

who go in and out of here year upon year of their loved one's incarceration. I watch a Hispanic family make their way through the metal detector. A boy of about five takes measured, deliberate steps through the contraption. His mother restrains his little brother from going through after him before he is given permission.

"Bridget." It's Buck Tooth calling me to the counter. He didn't call anyone else by their first name. Not even the regulars who come every week. I don't like him taking such liberty with me, but I choose to swallow my anger because I will not let this man get the better of me. Instead, I ask if he had a nice Thanksgiving and say mine was just dandy before gliding through the metal detector with a big grin on my face. "Being here is really the best part of the holiday," I add as he presses the inside of my wrist with the ultraviolet stamp.

It's natural that the guards wonder why any of us get involved with inmates, and I don't mind that since I, too, question my own actions. But there's something in Buck Tooth's gaze that suggests he is trying to figure out what is wrong with me. Yet, at the same time, I can tell that he thinks I am attractive and might be judging me a loser for visiting a prisoner. Like I should be with a guy like him, is what I read in his face. The truth is, I am not "with" any guy and I haven't been for a while and it is none of his business what I get out of visiting Rory.

So I say, "See you later," as sugary as I can, to Buck Tooth as he buzzes me through the door and into the first gated pen of the fences.

It's raining fairly hard and, since I assume umbrellas aren't allowed, I use my jacket to cover my head. Swiftly, I walk up the path and into the visiting building.

Inside the visiting room the blond guard with the striking

green eyes sits at the desk on the platform. She says, "It's nice to see you again," as I hand her my pass and then she assigns me to a table in the back corner. I say hello to Ruth at the vending machine and get coffee and orange juice. I comment on how cold the room is and she tells me the heat is broken. Great. I am wearing my favorite back-pleated skirt and festive red velvet top, which are not very warm. At least I am wearing boots.

I keep my jacket on, but the room is freezing and I put both my hands around the paper coffee cup. It's just about 9:30 when the first guys enter for their visits. Rory comes out around 9:50. Our morning kisses are just that, morning kisses, deep and loving but not passionate like the one that got Rory written up last time. I tell Rory that Buck Tooth is out in the processing center.

"Man, I went off on him," Rory says, about the last time when Buck Tooth reprimanded him for the kiss. "I said, 'Why don't you go and get that frickin' broken tooth of yours fixed, so you can go out and get your own girl and quit lookin' at mine!' " The write-up itself is not that big of a deal, but, since it's in his record, if something else happens they could use it to deny us visits.

"You didn't." I say.

"Hell, yeah, I did." Rory sits back in his chair and flicks the first two fingers on his right hand. "He ain't supposed to be lookin' at you."

We don't waste any more of our time talking about Buck Tooth.

Officer Green Eyes at the desk is one of Rory's favorites. The first time he ever saw her and she asked him to move something for her in the kitchen where he worked, Rory said "all-right," and did what she asked. Then he tells me he smiled at her and said, "And, no, I am not going to tell you you have gorgeous eyes!" He says they got along famously after that, because he was telling her that she was more than just her best feature.

He's always messing with people like that, saying something to take them off guard. "It trips people out when I say to someone, 'You know, you're real ugly,' or something like that, with a great big grin on my face!"

Rory's buoyancy always amazes me. That, and his ability to entertain himself even in prison when nothing is in his control. For instance, he planned to subtly and single-handedly change the prison lexicon. As it is, the usual interinmate greeting is a nod and an "all-right." Rory had told me on his first visit that he was going to start saying "o-kay" and gradually change the lingo.

When I ask how the project's progress is coming along he laughs, because he is stumped. "I keep trying different tones and intonations but I can't nail down the right 'o-kay' to use," he says. "But I'm not givin' up yet."

I ask about his writing. He's working on a new novel in which the main character has this ability to see what's inside of people, and through the colors they radiate he is able to heal them. "Women are almost always filled with a blue radiance from pain, which is almost always caused by a man," he explains. Even in his fiction, healing wounded women figures prominently.

I tell him about my "dates," not to make him jealous, but to show how he is healing me, freeing me up to even attempt dating again. The only part that makes him jealous is that he wants to be the one sitting with me when other couples say we look good together. He likes the pink coat story but, naturally, he wants to be the one opening the door.

He observes that my hands in his are still cold, but not

shaking so much. I sit facing him with our hands on top of the table and my shivering legs made warm between his under it. It's an embrace, not a sexual hold. If Buck Tooth were in the room he'd be all over us, but Green Eyes leaves us alone.

This time I don't feel the need to spill about my past pain and so I probe Rory about his. The story of his first memory almost breaks my heart. He was maybe three or four and his father was beating his mother and yelling at her. Rory first tried to hide in the closet but then felt ashamed that he wasn't helping his mother and he ran out of the house into the yard. They were living in Iowa at the time and it was winter. Barely able to see through his tears, Rory remembers finding in the slushy snow a small block of ice that encased one lone blade of grass.

"In my mind it is like the sun broke through the clouds in that instant, shining down on the blade of grass in the ice and the skies sang out 'a-ha,' " he says. "It was perfect, like a piece of glass with that one blade in it."

His little-boy eyes bore into the ice and on that perfect blade of grass, blocking everything else out of his head. He heard his father storm out and drive off. Then he went inside and found his mother making an ice pack for her brand-new set of bruises. He remembers going to put the grass-blade ice cube in with the others for her eye and she stopped him. "No, honey, that's for you," she said. She placed the perfect grass-blade ice cube in the freezer to preserve it. And Rory remembers the warmth of her body next to his as she snuggled with him in the big cushy chair in their living room, wrapped in a blanket with the ice pack on her face.

Just after the birth of his sister, Rory's father abandoned his mother with a broken pelvis. Rory says his mother and grandmother packed up all their things to drive back to California. His mother sat on an inflatable cushion and kept stopping to fill a cooler with ice along the way to keep that precious grass-blade ice cube safe.

"We kept that block of ice for years," he says, shaking his head, smiling a little at the memory of his mother caring for him. It finally melted during a power outage and Rory's memory of its thaw is entwined with the image of candle wax melting on a Monopoly board.

I have heard about this story before, but this is the first time he says it with such detail. Rory gives details like a novelist, but even if all of it cannot be true (I doubt, for instance, that his mother could've driven with a broken pelvis), it is clear that Rory witnessed his mother's abuse and abandonment, which contributed to his heightened sense of chivalry. Rory has told me other stories of other men abusing his mother. He stabbed one with a cheese knife because he was strangling his mother with the cord from the kitchen phone. Eventually, she left abusive men behind and found God, but then a leading pillar of the parish sexually abused Rory.

He wanted to run away, but where to?

Rory's father wasn't an option. He did an every-other-weekend thing with Rory and his sister, but that was about it. He married the woman he was having an affair with when he left Rory's mom and had a son with her.

With no other place to go, Rory ran away and lived with the family of a close friend. Unfortunately, the house was ruled by another abusive, alcoholic man. Now thirteen, no longer a child hiding in the closet, Rory stood up for the woman of the house this time and took the beatings himself. In reward for his gallantry she seduced him.

"I've never told anyone about that," he tells me. He had warned me that he wanted to share one of his biggest secrets with me on this visit, and I didn't know what to expect. I knew he had run away in his early teens and took up with a bunch of teenage drug dealers, and I knew he had been molested, but I didn't know the extent of the abuse. If Rory's ideas about chivalry and sex were not warped enough, now here was this woman who rewarded the boy's bravery with sex.

"I was happy that happened, actually," he tells me, "because after that guy in church I was afraid I might be gay." He was afraid to tell me about it because of my experience dealing with my ex-husband's abuse. He thought I might freak out and pull away from him.

I try to help him see how people who were supposed to take care of him abused him in some way: his father with abandonment and beatings; his mother with neglect and by exposing him to violent men; the church pedophile; and now this woman who used sex as a reward.

He resists judging his mother and says she did the best she could. "She didn't know about the church guy," he says. "And she didn't know what happened when I ran away." I'm thinking: Well, yes, technically, it's not her fault. But she did put him in that church, she didn't notice how he'd changed after the sexual abuse, and she didn't go after him when he ran away. I try to put a more gentle spin on my words, but that is what I think about his upbringing and I tell him he should be honest about it.

When he still resists, I don't push it.

I do press to find out just how old he was when he took to the street gang, but he says, "Time's weird for me, I get it confused." He also spent most of his youth in a drunken, doped haze, further complicating his memory. Eventually a bunch of the teenagers settled together in one of their father's homes, and Rory and his best friend Jon rose quickly to the top of the group's ranks.

This, however, was no social club.

I put this together with the rest of the story: how Rory fell for Jon's girl Amy, while Jon did a small jail stint; how she went back to Jon and crushed Rory's heart; how he fled to Reno to quit the scene and get clean; how after Jon's murder Amy called Rory, knowing full well about his need—no, addiction—to save women in distress. I know he killed partly because of his strong sense of chivalry and honor, which involved what he felt for both Jon and Amy.

I am not looking for rationalizations for his committing murder, and I never forget that Rory took someone's life. Still, I want to try and understand what was behind such violence. One of the biggest factors, I think, is that Rory didn't even think of life as being real.

"I thought I was Tony Montana," he says, adopting an Al Pacino *Scarface* accent. There is no pride in Rory's voice when he says this. Yet his crime was all about pride and the absolute uncontrollable need to stand up, be a man, and give Amy the revenge she wanted. Why else would he have told her to stay calm and wait for him to come back and take care of everything?

He admits that I might be right about that. He never wanted to blame someone else for his crime, though, because it doesn't do anything to bring back who he shot or change his own fate.

"I made this promise to myself that I would never kill again," he says, looking into my eyes. "But I don't know if I could keep that promise if something happened to you."

"You idiot. That is exactly why you are here," I want to scream, but simply say it in a low voice. "If something happened to me, if my man wanted to really take care of things and act like a man, then he'd take care of me, not go off and seek revenge." I tell Rory that I am upset by his remark, not impressed. "It's what you still need to learn."

"I'm working on it," he says. "I've never loved anyone like I love you."

"I know and I love you too, but . . ." I figure it's best to change the subject.

I imagine that Christmas in prison sucks, but Rory says that all the days pretty much suck about the same.

"I plan to keep my *It's a Wonderful Life* streak goin', though." Just because everyone tells him that it's the best movie, Rory has sworn to live his whole life without ever seeing it. I try to explain that he is probably depriving himself of something he might really like, especially with his heightened sense of romance.

"That's how being stubborn usually works," he says, which makes me laugh out loud. He tells me he loves my real laugh, and I feel lighter having used it.

As I drive back home, Rory's keen observation about being stubborn is what sticks out in my mind most about the visit. I told Rory I'd wear the same outfit I wore on the visit on Christmas Day and think of him when I am with my family in New Jersey. I don't even dread the holiday so much.

His Christmas card arrived the day before I left for the East Coast.

> *My Dearest Lovely Bridget . . .*
>> *I do not know what to say.*
>> *How can I free you and yet hold on so tight, so dearly to what you have created inside of me?*

So I will say only that I love you. Always you.

And my wish for you in this New Year is one of simple clarity. That you may see sharply and perfectly what it is you need to be truly happy in life, my love.

That you will show me, whether in person or in far away words, the smile of contentment, of safeness and final satisfaction. This is my ultimate hope for you. . . .

. . . And I believe this will start with the gift of clarity. For you must see and know and <u>define</u> [underlined twice] what it is that you desire to be able to reach for it.

And always know, never forget, never doubt, that I will forever be here for you. Forever love you.

Your Dark Knight,

Rory

Clarity. I liked that. I took the card with me when I went home for the holidays.

My parents and I spent an entire day together making enough homemade pasta to feed the family brood of about thirty expected to fill my parents' little retirement house to near-bursting on Christmas. I handled most of the physical part of the pasta-making process—mixing, kneading, and rolling out the dough. Dad's job was to grate the cheeses for the manicotti filling. And when it came time to cut and boil the dough we all got into the act. Then we formed an assembly line filling the dough squares and layering them with Mom's tomato sauce in trays. Near the end of the day, my mother said, "It feels like getting drunk without drinking."

Practically on cue, their neighbor Warren dropped by to

make martinis, as he does several times a week. I savored the routine of being in my parents' house.

My mother always woke up before everyone else so she could have her prayer time. I often woke up to find her sitting in my dad's La-Z-Boy with her prayer book. As others might do with recipes, my mother clipped prayers and kept them in a little bound book.

On Christmas Eve morning I found my mother exactly as I'd expected. She quickly finished her prayers, which I know without asking were often about me, and joined me for coffee in the kitchen. We've had many long conversations on those stools at that counter, my mother and me. This time she started off by telling me that I seemed to be in the best spirits I had been in in a long time.

"I just wish being in New Jersey at Christmas didn't remind me so much of all that I once had and hoped for here," I say, letting the tears fall. "What kills me is that Alexei never has to come back here and feel that loss."

"I'm mad at Alexei," my mother said. "He got away scot-free."

"But I am getting better, Mom. Christmas is just hard."

She already knew that I had been writing and visiting Rory, although I made it sound like it was all about my helping him get his writing published. I came clean with her that the relationship had a little more to it, but assured her that I wasn't going to go off and marry him. "He's begging me to let him lock away all of my pain," I said, crying tears of appreciation this time. "And I am. It's working. I'm finally letting some things go."

We stayed quiet for a bit and composed ourselves. "I know it's weird, Mom. But he's really helping me."

My mother had only one thing to say: "You never know who your angel is going to be."

———

That night my brother Patrick came over with his girlfriend, Andrea, and her grandmother for a preview of the pasta made for the next day. After Andrea and her grandmother went home, my parents, my brother, and I played the game of the house, Casino, on the kitchen counter until my mom got sleepy. The three of us continued to play until I got sleepy, and then we all went to bed.

In the middle of the night, Patrick's snores coming out of the twin bed next to mine drove me out to the couch in the living room. Cuddled up in a blanket I opened my eyes and found my mother in her usual place saying her prayers while it was still dark. Her voice wafted over me, an undecipherable, private, steady wave of sound.

I closed my eyes again, warmed by waking up on Christmas morning in my mother's prayers.

CHAPTER 8

KARA

On the yellowed pages of a 1973 yearbook from a San Bernardino high school named after some dead president are the smiling senior portraits of Kara and Jack. Nothing in the young classmates' faces foreshadows how they'd fall in love while sitting on opposite sides of Plexiglas at Pelican Bay State Prison more than twenty years later.

Kara looks like she could be my older cousin, with dark hair, pale skin, and sparkling blue-green Irish eyes. She's average height, on the slim side of shapely, and knows how to dress with style.

By the time Kara and I sit down to get her story on the record we already know each other a little—although I am not sure if "knowing" each other is really how I'd describe our relationship. Most friendships develop organically, based on mutual interests and circumstance. Since the circumstance among the visitor population is prison, it can complicate friendships formed there. The undercurrents of respect and reserve seem to help navigate visitors' interactions.

In some ways the prison factor acts like a shorthand in forming bonds based on similar experience, but then it also stands like a wall between people not wanting to expose too many of the details of their incarcerated loved one's business. This is especially true for gang members' families, who cannot divulge anything personal lest they invite retaliation for breaking the gang's code of silence.

Since neither Rory nor Jack is involved in a gang, Kara and I can communicate relatively freely. Still, we really stumbled into "knowing" each other. Both Kara and I visit the prison every few months, and it just so happened that several of our visits overlapped. Also, we both know Pamela, the wife of Rory's friend Pete, and so we've formed a sort of prison clique—taking walks together on the beach and going out to dinner after visiting. We don't really call or e-mail each other except to plan visit get-togethers. We like each other, that's clear, but it's not like we remember each other's birthdays.

Kara lives in Los Angeles, where she works as a manager for an upscale clothing retailer. Like me, she sometimes tacks her prison visits onto her business travels. When she was going to be in the San Francisco area for a meeting, she asked if I'd like to drive up with her on the weekend. I welcomed her company.

With the prison in on-again, off-again lockdown, we had a fifty-fifty chance of driving all the way up there only to be told we'd have just one hour to visit, behind glass. And there's always the risk the prison will go into complete lockdown and visiting will be canceled altogether. That's just part of prison life.

It's a typical drizzling February day when I pick Kara up at a shopping mall near my home in Oakland. As always, she looks great: dressed stylishly as befits her years of fashion experience. She's a very young and polished fifty-one. Since Jack's near the end of his time, she's hoping this might be her last visit to Pelican Bay.

As people tend to do on road trips, we tell each other our lives. Kara and Jack grew up together. "Our families mirrored each other," she says, meaning both big Irish families had several kids of the same age and in the same grades at school. Despite being in the same class, Jack and Kara never dated in school.

"He was very shy, mostly because of his upbringing," she explains. "His father was nutso."

Even though visitors are careful about revealing their inmates' information, often we already know something about their business through the inmates we visit. When Kara calls Jack's father "nutso," I assume she is referring to the father's shooting the mother before turning the gun on himself when Jack was thirteen.

"It didn't kill her; I guess it was a small-caliber gun. But he hit himself in such a way that it killed him instantly," she tells me.

"Was Jack there?" I ask.

"No, but the kids were all farmed out to neighbors and family." Jack always felt responsible for what happened to his mother. And his father had spent most of his living days drunk, yelling at Jack about how worthless he was. "He never really thought he had much going for himself," Kara continues. "So when someone offered him heroin one time, he took it, and it made him feel like a million bucks. His pain went away, and all of his fears and everything. He said it was instantaneously his drug of choice."

Within a few years Jack started to steal to get his fix. He was twenty-two when he went to prison for armed robbery. He got twelve years and served ten.

Kara spent that time getting married and starting a family.

She lived in Arcata, and when we get up to that part of Interstate 101, she points out the very house she lived in with her family. It's far off the freeway, on a hill, overlooking the ocean. She delivered mail and indicates the places up and down the coast of Humboldt County where she had her routes. We are driving through her past.

Nestled safe in her world, just two hours away from Pelican Bay—never even dreaming that one day she'd be involved with a prisoner there—Kara marched on with a life that seemed on track. Until someone told her that her husband was having an affair.

"And she told me exactly where he was at that moment with the woman," says Kara. "So I hopped in the car with my youngest daughter in the backseat and drove down and caught him at a motel." She found him outside of San Francisco, and points out where a state trooper pulled her over, late that night more than fifteen years ago, when she sped back up to Arcata to pack up the pieces of her shattered life. Seeing how shaken she was, and after hearing what had happened, the officer didn't give her a ticket. "He didn't have the heart," says Kara, "but he looked in the backseat and saw my daughter sleeping there and said, 'But you've got someone else to consider.'" She pauses with a blank look on her face and canvasses the area before speaking again.

"It was good to be reminded of that, just then." It's almost as if she recalls the incident with fondness, perhaps grateful another human being witnessed her hour of greatest despair. She'll never know his name or his badge number, but she'll never forget that intimate moment with a stranger on a dark stretch of highway.

Meanwhile, Jack did his time and got out. Right away, his stepfather helped him land a job in a landscaping business.

"Everything was going great. And he picked up with an old flame and they were living together," Kara continues. "He looked good, he was lifting weights. He was up to 225, and had a great upper body.

"Even his parole officer was telling him he was doing great. And he felt he had to keep up this persona, to be the success story for everyone," says Kara. Then his work led to back pain and when his sister gave him a Vicodin, snap! "He was like, whoa, here's that euphoric feeling from way back and it took the pain away," Kara explains. "This is the kind of guy . . . He took the whole bottle and then he went back to the doctor and got some more, you know." That started Jack's backsliding and it didn't take long for him to seek out his drug of choice, thinking, as addicts do, that he could handle it.

Jack hung out with one of Kara's brothers, who was a drug addict at the time. She says even he warned Jack about scoring some heroin. "He was like, don't even go down that road," she remembers. Quickly, Jack developed a thousand-dollar-a-day habit and headed back down the armed robbery path to feed it.

The last time Kara saw Jack outside of prison walls was at their twentieth high school reunion. She was divorced and had settled in Southern California with her three children to be near her family. She remembers the reunion well.

"We had a few dances and I knew he was strung out on heroin," she remembers. "My girlfriend and I drove him to the place, a hotel, he was staying at. The police were looking for him and it was close to the end. He was sitting in the backseat and I said, 'You better get your life together, buddy, you're really blowin' it.' And he said, 'Yeah, yeah, I will.'" Within a month or two, the police caught him in the process of robbing a jewelry store.

"Red-handed, huh?" I say.

"When they cuffed him he just said, 'Thank God, thank God, it's over,' because he knew he was out of control and he couldn't do anything about it." Jack got twenty-five years, which at the time meant he'd likely serve half of it. (If California's "Three Strikes and You're Out" law were in effect then, he would have gotten life.)

As Kara worked her way up the management ladder at her retail job, Jack dove into "prison politics," which is lingo for violence, usually fueled by racial tension. "He was in and out of the SHU, which means he must have been involved in incidents where people got injured," says Kara. "He was never violent before—even when he armed robbered, he never hurt anybody and he felt bad about it. He just needed his drugs." She says Jack lost himself in prison.

When Kara found him again he was in the SHU. She had no intention of getting involved with him. Jack's mother had worked for Kara one holiday season, and she innocently asked which prison Jack wound up in. When his mother said he was at Pelican Bay, Kara remembered hearing about the prison being built back when she lived in Arcata. Since she still went up there from time to time, she suggested she might go say "hi" to Jack. A few months later she kept her word.

Visits to the SHU are by appointment only, and Kara was given a two-and-a-half-hour slot. "I told my friend who drove me there that I'd probably end up talking to him for about an hour or so," Kara remembers. "Two and a half hours later, we were still talking."

Within the first few seconds, however, Kara knew that he'd changed drastically. "It was so sad when I saw his face. He was such a dashing man when I saw him before—no gray, no nothing," she says. "He was like, weathered. And his eyes . . . It was like there was no softness and he didn't trust anybody."

Instead of being happy to see Kara, Jack called her a "do-gooder" and wanted to know why the hell she came to see him. It took a little while, but Kara says he began to relax and open up. "I broke through the ice a little, and I just didn't have the heart to get up and leave," she adds. So she stayed the whole time and told him it was okay if they wrote to each other. "He looked at me straightaway and said, 'I'm not talking shallow, little stuff, but to really share on deep levels.' " Kara agreed. She also made it clear that nothing else was going to happen between them. That was seven years ago.

"But I could tell by the third letter that he was very interested, and that he thought I was super-duper, and he doesn't know why men didn't want to commit to me in the past." At the time, Kara says dating had grown tiresome for her and that she called it a "rat race" when she wrote back to Jack. He wrote that he couldn't understand the fools who didn't see how beautiful she is.

"Well, he's not wrong there," I say. "Rory's got a little crush on you."

This makes her laugh heartily. "He's so young."

"It's a good thing I'm not the jealous type," I say, laughing with her. "Rory says you're the kind of woman who gets better looking every day."

Her laughs give way to a sigh. "Yeah, but guys out there aren't willing to commit. I mean, what's not to love here?"

She shakes her head and gets back to the story of Jack and Kara. Very early on Jack sent her a poem he wrote about a hummingbird hovering over another grievously wounded bird. "It was beautiful," says Kara. "But I knew what he was saying. He wanted me to be the hummingbird, coming in there bringing him comfort and love. And I said, 'No, no, no, no, no. I'm not going to be your rescuer.' "

"I guess you weren't the do-gooder he accused you of," I say.

"It hurt his feelings," she says. "But I told him he had to get healin' on his own."

The next time Kara planned to visit her friends in Arcata, she called the sergeant in charge of visiting at Pelican Bay and requested more time with Jack. Since she was coming from Southern California and could not visit often, he granted Jack and Kara two full visiting days. Plexiglas stood between them, but they used the time to come together and sort out their relationship. Not that it's ever been easy.

"A lot of times we'd fight and he'd say, 'Just go then, and leave me to rot.' There were a lot of childish episodes." She understood that Jack never dealt with the emotional fallout from his childhood, and the violent climax of his father's final act. Even still, she made it clear to him that she was not his savior and that he'd have to work on his stuff before their relationship could be more than a friendship. "I had my stuff, too, from my marriage," she says.

Jack worked to expand his mind through reading literature of all kinds, but mostly he wanted to educate himself about psychology. "He said, 'I gotta go into these dark rooms and figure it out,' " she says. "It scared him to death, but he finally wanted to live a healthy life and get out of that hellhole." When he was released back into the prison's general population, Jack steered clear of politics. He found his true calling in the Reaching Out Convicts to Kids, or ROCK, program.

A few times a year, a handful of teenage boys who are more than just teetering toward a criminal future are brought into

Pelican Bay to interact with the ROCK inmates. Becoming a ROCK inmate isn't easy. First, the prison staff sift through the applications looking for inmates who they think will interact in a positive way with the boys. Then the prisoners selected rate one another. There are seven inmates on the ROCK team and Jack's been a participant for six years.

"When he gets talking about those kids, he's so passionate," says Kara.

More than a scared-straight program, ROCK aims to engage kids. The inmates show them the realities of prison life—the shanks, the cells, the rules, the sorrow. They talk honestly with the kids about their mistakes and addictions that landed them behind bars, some of them for life.

"With budget cuts, they're not bringin' them in so much, but every single time Jack gets through to the kids by the end of the day. Because they are like him, broken," says Kara. She's clearly proud of Jack's work with ROCK and appreciates how it pumps him up and helps him develop a sense of worth. "He says that if these twenty years of hell could be used to help kids, then it wouldn't be wasted." She adds that when Jack tells a kid, one-on-one, that he doesn't have to be a big man and he can cry, it really gets to him.

Jack plans to continue working with kids when he gets out, and Kara wants to be right beside him doing something worthwhile. "We both have that compassion for children who are just innocent victims of parents who shouldn't be parents," she says. "I see us on a ranch where you can really, every day, work with the kids and just love on 'em."

Learning how to love well has been the centerpiece of Jack and Kara's seven years together. Although it's not always been a smooth ride.

She laughs as she tells me the story now, but five years ago, when she refused his wish for her to become his healer yet again, he came at her "with everything he had." He blasted her, screaming venomous words that accused her of betraying him. All the other visitors in the room stared at them. The guard walked by their table and that stopped Jack's tirade. "I told him, I'm never going to be with a man who's abusive, or where he has fits of anger and goes off the Richter scale. I'm outta here if you don't start dealing with your stuff." Then she walked out. When he called her later, she said, "You can't act like a child and treat people like that," and she hung up. He called back. Click. Called again. Click.

Eventually she talked with him and told him point-blank: "I'm walking this with you. I'm trying here, but you've got to get it together." That drove him, and Jack became brutally honest about his raw thoughts and feelings as he processed his childhood traumas and adult mistakes. He poured it out in almost daily letters to Kara. "He said, 'I'm broken, but please don't think I'm too broken.'" What impressed her then, and impresses her still about Jack, is his openness and willingness to communicate about what is truly going on in his heart. "Most guys are so protected and closed," she says. "These guys in there have nothing to lose and they are dying to connect."

"And it sounds like you were starved for a connection," I interject.

"Exactly," she says. "But he helps me with my stuff, too."

Jack called Kara on her own guarded heart right from the start of their relationship. "He told me, 'You have your armed guards and your walls are high,'" she says. "When my husband left me I was devastated, and I never really trusted men. And I wasn't good at relationships." She thinks part of her trouble with men stems back to growing up in a frank "no-holds-barred kind

of family." She admits now that she said and did things in relationships without thinking, which pushed people away. When
she did this with Jack, he didn't pull away. "He'd say, 'You've got
to temper some of that come-attcha stuff.' " She agreed, despite
herself. "I saw that it wasn't a good quality in me. So, we've both
helped each other."

But three years ago, she broke Jack's heart when she agreed
to marry him and then backed out of it at the last minute.

"One time I was up there he just kept asking me and asking
me. And he kinda broke me down. I mean, I was committed to
him, so I finally said yes and he was thrilled," Kara explains. "But
that was part of wanting to control me." She knew his buddies
inside were pushing him because, since Jack wasn't a lifer, they
could have conjugal visits if they were married. "It's part of the
dynamic with those guys," she says, lowering her voice for effect.
"It's like, 'You gotta get your girl in line, you know. You gotta get
her to doin' your deal.' "

She talked with her pastor about the marriage when she got
back home, and he begged her not to do it. "It was already what
I knew in my heart of hearts; that I had gotten away from myself," she says. "He called and I was kinda cavalier about it. I was,
so, honey, I just can't do it."

"On the phone?" I ask, unable to hide my surprise.

"Oooooooh, I didn't realize how devastating it would be. But
that was part of the cold and callousness I had to work on."

Jack told Kara not to come back after the wedding bow-out,
but she returned anyway. She needed to try to help him understand her side of it; even if she handled it terribly, she still loved
him. She says she wanted to marry him and had even gone so far
as getting the license. But she couldn't tell her family, even her
daughters, who fully supported her relationship with Jack.

"He needed to understand that I just didn't want to go to one of those family visiting houses and do it for the first time," Kara continues. She told him she would be getting married for his convenience and losing herself in the process. He listened to her, but she knew he was devastated. To make things worse, that same weekend, another couple exchanged wedding vows in the visiting room. "It still hurts him to talk about it. To this day, he's said, 'I have processed it and I understand, but the hurt caused at the time was very, very intense.' "

Kara knows Jack felt humiliated. "Even if those guys may not be who he'd choose as friends, they are his friends," she explains. It doesn't help Jack's wounded ego when the lifers—who obsess about the conjugal visits they will never have—remind him that his lady didn't come through for him. "But we came through it, and I gotta give him credit for that," she says.

It has taken Kara and Jack years to build their relationship, and she says she doesn't regret it "one iota." Even the time apart is made bearable by the intense connection they have now. "He has such wonderful compassionate gifts. And he's free to express himself. I'm the recipient of this great love he's learned to give and it's beautiful," she concludes.

It seems like a good place to pause the interview as we coast down the forested last leg of the trip and into Crescent City.

We arrive at a motel at about 9:30 p.m. Since I covered the gas for the trip, Kara arranged for the accommodations at her motel of choice located right on the ocean. We each pick a bed and settle down for the night.

"Oh, I have something for you," says Kara. And she goes into her bag and takes out a cute cropped corduroy jacket, the kind that everyone seems to be wearing.

Her thoughtfulness touches me, and I tell her I will wear it tomorrow. We spend the evening watching *What Not to Wear* on The Learning Channel. It's her favorite TV show.

We easily get ready together the next morning. I do wear the off-white jacket over a black flowing skirt and black top accented with a long strand of freshwater pearls, which I double. Kara wears a turquoise jacket that makes her eyes shine even brighter than they normally do and cuffed, cropped slacks that are in style. All of her toiletries are in neat matching bags and containers. Mine are thrown in a plastic grocery-store bag. All I've brought by way of makeup products are the foundation, mascara, and lipstick I always carry in my purse. When Kara offers to do my makeup with her supplies, I'm all for it. I can't even remember the last time I wore blush or eye shadow.

We sit by the window overlooking the ocean so Kara can use the natural morning light to apply the makeup. "I'm just so tired of this," she says, meaning the years of visiting.

"I bet you are," I say, thinking to myself that there's no way I am going to let that be my future.

Part of why Kara, Pamela, and I could even become friends is because our guys all get along—for the most part. Jack moved to Rory and Pete's tier just that week, so they are all neighbors now. Pete fancies himself a prison preacher and that gets on everyone's nerves from time to time.

After one visit Pete sent me a letter, by way of Rory. He meant well; he could see that I was clearly going through some challenges in my life. His letter called me to be born again in Christ. He told me his mission in life is to bring people to God and that he only wanted to help me. He included some material on being saved, which I didn't read beyond the first sentence. I wrote back—again by way of Rory, because I didn't want Pete to have my address. I tried to be nice for Pamela's sake, and I also didn't want to cause a rift between Pete and Rory, because they are stuck together on the same tier. Still, I firmly told Pete that while I respected his mission he was not invited into my personal relationship with God. He backed off after that, but ever since, I sense something beneath his saccharine greetings to me, as if he thinks it's just a matter of time before he gets through to me.

Rory insists Pete's not so bad, and that his intentions are good and his motive sincere. Sometimes he just has a hard time hearing no.

As we drive to the prison, I share these thoughts about Pete with Kara. It turns out she feels the same way. And she, too, stifles her feelings for both Pamela's and Jack's sake. "He drives Jack nuts sometimes," she says. "But then Jack also tries to reach out to him."

When Kara and I get to the prison we learn that it's still on lockdown because of rampant racial violence, mostly between the northern and southern Californian Mexican gangs. Instead of canceling all contact visits—the kind where the inmates can sit at a table in the visiting room—the warden decided to stagger them by race. Black and white inmates are allowed on alternating weekends, and the same goes for northern and southern Mexicans. Lucky for us, the warden decided to allow white contact visits first. The people visiting black inmates are told to make appointments for one-hour slots, which will be behind glass.

Pamela explains all of this as we wait to be processed.

In February, the rainy season, when the driving in northern California can be treacherous, the visiting room is never very full. With the absence of blacks and many Latinos, this time it's almost empty, with only four other tables occupied besides Kara's, Pamela's, and mine.

Our three guys come out together, in the middle of sharing some joke.

"Jack's a nut," Rory says as he sits down, shaking his head in affectionate disbelief, looking over at Jack and Kara. He tells me how Jack, who has severe OCD, scrubbed and scrubbed his new cell all week. "And last night he was obsessing that he knows 'the neurons' are still there lurking in the corner," says Rory.

I ask Rory how he thinks Jack is going to do when he gets out. "That's why I wanted to move him near me," Rory says. "So I could help him." Rory says Jack's scared and is starting to mess up, even getting drunk sometimes. "But Kara isn't going to take his crap," he says confidently. "He knows he's a lucky guy, he's just scared." He tells me that a lot of guys who are at the end of their sentences mess up before they get out. Rory invited Jack to start working out with him, thinking it might ease his stress.

For fifty-one, he says Jack's been keeping up pretty well with the regimen of squats, burpees, and push-ups, though it's only been a few days since they've started.

When we walk past their table to go get some food out of the vending machines, Rory says to Jack, "The neurons! The neurons!" Jack throws his head back and laughs at himself. Kara is laughing with him, and I guess he has already told her about the condition of his new cell and how it is driving him crazy.

I like the idea of these guys having each other in there, even if they get on one another's nerves. Pete's preaching might be annoying, but I also know he'd have their backs if they needed him.

We're not supposed to cross-visit, but Pete calls me "Johnny Cash" every time we're near each other because of my black boots, skirt, and shirt. I decide to forgive him the saccharine smile that comes with the comment.

We all enjoy this kind of rare interaction, but we keep it to a minimum, more out of respect for the other couples' precious time alone than an urge to follow prison rules.

Kara goes home with Pamela after the visit because she is staying with her for the night. Pamela asked me to stay as well, but I know I need some alone time. Besides, I like my regular Travelodge room. We plan to meet later for dinner at Pamela's favorite place, an Italian bistro. As usual, we eat early and are the first table seated that evening.

We talk about our jobs and our families. Pamela takes me by surprise when she suggests we go see *Brokeback Mountain*. For an evangelical Christian, it seems an unlikely choice, but I figure she might not know what the movie is about and is just reacting to all the hype around it.

"I already saw it," I say. "Um, do you know what it's about?" She shakes her head. I give a brief description. They know some of my history and so I tell them how I went to see the movie, by myself, on New Year's Day. Rory planted the idea of making New Year's themes instead of resolutions and that year I chose "no ghosts, no fears" as my theme. The hype about *Brokeback Mountain* resurrected the ghost of my marriage. And the scant attention paid to the women in news articles about "brokeback marriages" infuriated me. To be fair, I tell them, I thought they handled the wives' roles well in the movie.

"It's one of the saddest movies I've ever seen," I tell them.

How could I have seen it any other way? It made me stew about some things in my marriage. I tell them my theory that while I thought the one character was clearly gay, for the other guy it seemed like the sex was something he stumbled into. Ennis was so damaged by his childhood. He was confused. He reminded me of Alexei.

Since seeing the film, I fought an urge to call Alexei. The movie made me wonder if Alexei experienced some sort of encounter with a man before I moved out. He had told me he never cheated on me, but now I am not so sure. I thought back to a road trip he took with classmates from grad school during winter break when they drove to another art school in another state. They stayed in motels along the way. I didn't give it a thought then, but now I wonder if something sexual happened and Alexei enjoyed it. He was never quite the same after he got back from that trip. Did I want to confront him about that now, when for the past year I had purposely not had any contact with him for the first time since we met in 1987?

My stomach churns as I talk about it with Kara and Pamela. When Pamela, ever the warmhearted one, suggests we rent a different movie to watch at her house, I decline. I feel bad about having taken the conversation in that personal direction, even if they both listened and offered me their comfort and support. I think it's better for me to stay in my little room and read until I fall asleep.

"Even I get tired of my story," I say to Kara the next day, after visiting, and as we head out on our drive back down 101. "Honestly, just when I think I've made real progress, something like *Brokeback Mountain* comes along."

I reach for my tape recorder in the compartment between the seats and say, "Shall we continue with you?"

She starts by telling me that her father went to meet Jack a few years after Kara started going out with him. Or in this case, it's more like going in with him, I guess. Anyway, Kara says her father, who knew Jack as a kid and knew his history, asked him if he was all done with drugs and the criminal life. This gave Jack the chance to explain man-to-man that he loved his daughter, that she was the best thing that had ever happened to him, and that he would never hurt her. "It meant a lot to him to have that conversation, even though my father was old and feeble," says Kara.

"What did your mother think?"

"When I first told my mother she made me feel worthless for being involved with an inmate," she says. Kara's parents have been divorced for years. "She said, 'He's going to kill you!' She was just on me all the time." Kara says her mother knew Jack's father had killed, and she wouldn't let Kara forget about that. Understandably, Kara is much closer with her father than her mother. "Jack says my mother is a bitter old woman," she says.

If others in her family disapprove of her relationship with Jack, they keep it to themselves. "My daughters hope for the best because I have been alone for a very long time," she says. One of her sisters says the whole experience has made Kara a more humble person.

"To go into a visiting room like that," Kara says, "yeah, I would've judged them as a bunch of idiots, to put all their eggs in that basket." She thinks differently now. She says Jack likes to think he's better than Pete, who Jack thinks gave Pamela a life sentence when he married her. "I remind him that he got me on the line when he was facing nine more years. It hasn't been easy for me and he's no better."

Kara says that lately she has noticed a sadness in Pamela. On the last visit when we were all together, Pamela met up with us after going to a wedding on the reservation where her extended family lives. It was the first and only time either of us had seen her cry. Just a few months before, Pamela couldn't even visit Pete for their anniversary because the prison was on total lockdown.

"But Pete does something for her that we don't understand," says Kara.

"I guess so," I say. "I just think she doesn't have much in her life here besides Pete. I sense that she'd like to be with her family on the reservation but then she might not get to visit Pete every weekend."

"She's made lots of sacrifices, as I have," says Kara.

"Do you ever feel cheated?" I ask.

"No. He's so affectionate, and I've never had that." Kara and her husband were sexual but not intimate. They never held hands. "Jack and I don't even like to be around each other without touching. And I need all those loving strokes.

"For fifty-one years we've lived in isolation of intimacy," she continues. "When you can feel comfortable and let your hair down with this person and you can be totally exposed and secure as we are together—we built that. I've never had that with anyone else. And I don't think it could've happened any other way, because we both needed those years to work on what's wrong with us."

She anticipates my next question without my asking it. "Neither one of us are scared about when he gets out," she declares. "He's been in prison all these years, and we know there are going to be a lot of adjustments, but he knows this is his last chance."

"The neurons! The neurons!" I say, making us both laugh at Jack's OCD, just one of the "things" they'll have to deal with when he gets out. Kara's laughing so hard she nearly spills coffee on herself.

"We're still on the journey and I think we will be on it a long time," she says after a few minutes. She starts laughing again because Jack warned her earlier today that he's going to take her to a Rolling Stones concert and to NASCAR.

"What will you wear to NASCAR?" I ask.

Her laughter rises an octave, in a girlish, oh-what-we-do-for-love kind of way.

Her attitude reminds me of how I finally gave in to my feelings for Rory two years earlier.

CHAPTER 9

CAGED DREAMS

Once I drove through nine rainbows to get to prison.
This thought pops into my head as I count the number of rainbows I pass on my way to visit Rory on the New Year's Eve weekend after my mother said, "You never know who your angel is going to be." As writers, Rory and I often try out opening lines on each other from stories we are writing or want to write. It doesn't matter if we actually wind up using the lines; we simply enjoy playing with words together. I know Rory is going to love the image of nine rainbows when I tell him about it tomorrow, because he's always looking for things that connect us, like our double-nine birthdays. The latest connection was when we both, unbeknownst to the other, zoned out while listening to the same tape (Madonna's *The Immaculate Collection*) after our last visit around Thanksgiving.

"C'mon," he said sarcastically on the phone after that visit. "Yeah, Madonna's real popular in a men's prison."

Where I see a coincidence, Rory sees something more. We do try to connect by reading the same books or watching the same movies. Recently he'd asked me to watch one of his favorite films, *What Dreams May Come.* It stars Robin Williams and

Annabella Sciorra as a married couple who lose their two children in a car accident. After Robin Williams's character dies, most of the movie takes place in his personal heaven, where he meets up with the souls of his mentor and his children, although he does not recognize them. In her grief on earth, his wife takes her own life. Williams sets out to save his soul mate from an eternity in darkness and finally realizes it is his son who helps him in this impossible task. It's a sweet story about soul mates and universal connections between them, but as much as I like the idea, I remain skeptical.

I credit science for the rainbows. But nine of 'em? I'll let Rory read whatever he wants into that phenomenon. I know our hearts connect us, but we still occupy separate worlds, and if coincidences make him feel closer to me and more alive, why not let him have them?

Another holiday weekend at Pelican Bay. Every year the prison adds an extra visiting day on the weekend closest to five selected holidays, which brings more families than usual to the prison to take advantage of the extra time with their incarcerated loved ones. Work prevented me from leaving until Friday, so when I arrive at prison on Saturday morning, most of the visitors waiting in the packed processing center are back for day two of three. I say hello to Ruth as we cross paths—me on my way to the desk to fill out a pass, she on her way to the ladies' room. She wears a jingle bell around her neck instead of the necklace Burnard made for her in the eyeglass shop.

This time the sergeant recognizes me—I guess I'm becoming a regular—and asks about my holidays when he takes my pass and ID to be processed. He tells me I look almost too good for going in there, and I realize that he was the guard from my first visit who made me cut the underwire out of my bra and let me bypass the metal detector when we discovered that my buttons were setting it off.

I smile as I leave the counter and walk toward where Pamela is sitting with several women I do not know. She introduces me, but they seem to be in the middle of a discussion about changes in prison procedure regarding packages they can send to sons and lovers inside. Families used to be able to send packages of food, toiletries, writing supplies, and other prison-approved items directly to the inmates at several prison-approved times a year. But too much contraband, i.e., drugs, was getting through. Now the families have to order materials from a company chosen by the prison to fulfill them—at a higher cost.

No one is happy about it, but they can't do much except comply. Ruth overhears the conversation and stops to tell them that the family council, in which she participates and whose members meet monthly to discuss inmate and family grievances, is planning to discuss the package issue with the assistant warden. She urges the women—especially those who live far away and cannot attend family council meetings—to drop their ideas in the suggestion box in the back of the room next to a clipboard mounted on the wall. I've checked out the clipboard before; it contains the minutes to family council meetings. The perpetual issues seem to be the high cost of collect calls, slow mail, inmates getting the proper depression medication (especially in the SHU), and now the packages.

I notice that the woman Pamela introduced me to as Naomi isn't following the conversation and so I go stand near where she is sitting. Naomi's Native American, like Pamela, but from a different tribe. She tells me there are two sizable reservations about an hour-and-a-half drive southeast near Eureka and that she lives on one of them with her children and grandchildren. I want to say that she looks too young to have grandchildren but do not want to pry.

I've found that the safest thing to ask when meeting another visiting woman is how she met the inmate she visits. Naomi says she met her husband through her cousin who is married to an inmate. "I never—" she starts to say, but the guard cuts her off by calling her up to the counter. I suspect she was going to say she never thought she'd get involved with an inmate in a million years. It's the common refrain, what they all say. It's what I say, too.

I take Naomi's seat next to an elderly woman who is twisting what looks like a sapphire ring on her left hand. She is dressed in a neat, comfy, retirement-community way. She wears dark slacks, a pastel blouse, and a white sweater. She seems to want to be left alone, and so I turn my attention to the black woman across the aisle who is trying to keep her little girl and boy to her side.

"They look so festive," I say, noting the girl's green-and-red ribbon and the boy's reindeer sweater.

"More like feisty," she says good-naturedly, but not exactly in a way that invites more conversation. Most of the women with children keep to themselves; perhaps they have enough on their hands managing to get their kids to behave in that setting, or simply want to protect their privacy.

Great, I think, I'm turning into one of those childless women who coo over every cute kid she sees.

"Polizzi," the guard calls out and the elderly woman next to me gets up. It's Rory's celly's last name. This must be Tony's mother, I think. Rory had mentioned that she might come for this weekend, but Tony hadn't been able to get through to her on the phone to confirm.

By the time I am processed through and make my way into

the visiting room (where, thankfully, Officer Buck Tooth is not present), most of the tables are already filled. A couple of guards are setting up extra tables and chairs from those stored in the back corner to accommodate the expected arrival of yet more families. The officer seated on the platform assigns me a table near the television and children's play area.

With so many visitors, it takes extra time for the guys to come out, and I worry that Rory won't make the 10:30 count cutoff. As I walk to the vending machines, a black inmate I have seen before but never spoken with says, "Oh, he's comin'. It's just takin' a while." His girlfriend turns to look at me and I say "thank you" in a way that addresses both of them, because I am not so sure she likes her man taking notice of me. Besides, we sit on our own private islands at these tables and I do not wish to intrude on their time.

So I get my coffee, go back to my table, and mind my own business.

Tony's mother is sitting a couple of tables over from me, kitty-corner, and I contemplate introducing myself. She is in profile, clutching her sweater closed at her bosom as she watches the clock behind the officer's platform. Unsure of the protocol, I decide not to bother her.

Tony and Rory have lived in the same cell together for five years. "It's the longest relationship I've ever had," Rory once joked. Both lifers, Rory has described their bond as a brotherhood. He has also told me that Tony's mom tells people that her son lives out west and fights forest fires.

Even though I have never seen Tony, I can guess it's him when he comes out by his macho strut. Real firefighters don't need to strut, I think, the uniform does it for them. I knew Tony was on the short side, like Rory, because they sometimes wore each other's clothes. Tony's thinner, looks about my age, and is not as buff as Rory. From what Rory's said about Tony's ego, he'd hate it if I thought Rory was in better shape. He has short, thinning brown hair and wears extended sideburns that are not quite to the point of being classified as pork chops.

Tony and his mother engage in a stiff, quick embrace at first, but then he pulls her tightly into his arms. "Hey, Ma," I hear him say. When they walk toward the vending machines, I follow.

"Well, hello, Bridget," says Tony in a tone that means, Oh, yeah, I know who you are.

"Guess you've seen enough pictures of me, huh?" I say.

He introduces me to his mother, who I learn has traveled from Florida where she lives with one of her daughters. "Tony's my baby," she says. Her wavy, white shoulder-length hair frames her face and I see tears sitting on the rims of her blue eyes. I try to lighten the mood by saying that even at forty my parents insist on calling me their baby, too. It seems to work, and she tells me how she hasn't been able to come here for about a year to see Tony. I leave them at their island and go back to my own to wait for Rory.

I jump inside a little each time I hear the clang of keys on the other side of the door the prisoners come through.

Rory comes out just minutes before the 10:30 count. He's grown his hair out, as I asked him to. He stops to say hello to Mrs. Polizzi first, before coming over to me. Tony pushes him on, saying, "You've got somebody waitin' over there." Rory says, "Yeah, yeah." And I think this is a pretty common interaction for them: Tony telling Rory what to do, and Rory doing just what he pleases.

Using his own Rory strut, he stretches his arms out wide as he makes his way toward me, like he is getting ready to embrace the world. "Happy New Year, pretty girl," he says before nearly swooping me off the ground in his arms as he kisses me hello.

"Man, I just want to pick you up and twirl you around!" he says.

"I like the hair," I say, giving it a good tousle.

He brushes it back and his lopsided grin falls into a frown. He laments how it is not growing in nearly as thick as he remembered on top, and that what is coming in is more gray than black. "I used to wear it long. The girls loooooved it," he says, his grin coming back. "And I had this widow's peak. For Halloween, I'd be Dracula every year."

"What is it with boys and Halloween?" I ask as he takes my hands in his, the touch of his skin making me feel most at home in my own. I tell him about my Christmas trip back east and waking up to my mother's prayers.

"You are very much your mother's daughter, my love." With his sweet words floating in the air, our hands entwined, suddenly it doesn't even feel like we are in that room anymore. Tony, Pete, the guards, and the smell of popcorn all disappear. Even the fluorescent lights seem to dim when he drinks in the features of my face and pushes my hair out of my eyes. I am looking down at our hands as he does this, and I can feel his leg trembling next to mine beneath the table.

"I wish there was a word other than beautiful for you," he says in a whisper.

When I look up and into his eyes I think the kind of love I see there is what George Harrison must have felt when he wrote the song "Something." "And all I have to do is think of her . . ." The lyrics alone convey love. But the magic of the song lies in the melding of beautiful words with a guitar refrain that is the essence of a lover's embrace made audible.

"I wish I could make time stop, and freeze everyone in place, and just hold you," Rory says.

"You are holding me."

When Tony comes by, I am not sure how much time has lapsed. He is leading his mother over to the seats in front of the TV, which puts them right next to us.

"So how'd you like the hair, Bridget?" he asks. "That's all I've heard about since the last time you were here. He's like a girl. 'Should I shave it? It's so thin.' He's been driving me nuts."

Rory grins and leans back in his chair with his arms folded. He shrugs and says, "We're like a married couple."

"Do you like it?" repeats Tony.

"Yes, I do," I say, smiling, giving it another tousle.

"There, you hear that? That's the end of that," he says. Tony speaks with a grousing intimacy, which I think is just part of his shtick in their relationship. Rory, Mr. Sensitive, and Tony the Hothead. They do act like a married couple. Tony's a little too pushy and gruff for me to want to spend a lot of time with him, but they clearly get along, and I am happy Rory has more than a celly—a real brother—in there.

"Hey, did you ask her about that Washington stuff?" Tony asks Rory.

"Give me time, bro, we just got out here."

"Dude, it's one o'clock in the afternoon." He shakes his head and murmurs, "You two . . . Ask her, willya?"

Tony wants me to find out if lifers in Washington State get family visits. Rory explains that Tony's girlfriend, whom he met when she worked as a supervisor in the laundry, quit her job

so that she could visit Tony out here. They'd hidden their relationship for several months, because if they had been caught,
she'd have gotten fired at the very least and might even have
been arrested and sent to prison.

Rory says it's better if we do not know the specifics about
Tony and his girlfriend Stella's relationship. He says it's the first
time Tony's been in love. I assume they were sneaking sex but
chose a legitimate relationship over a physical one. To achieve
that, Stella quit her job so they could start writing to each other.
Now she is waiting to become an approved visitor.

Meanwhile, Tony's making plans. Rory explains that Tony
wants to get transferred to Washington, where, if they were married, he and Stella might have conjugal visits. Rory says it's a
fiction Tony conjures up for himself, to dream of something even
as a lifer. Much in the same way Rory dreams in his novels, I think.

At the end of the visit, I tell Tony that I'll look into Washington for him. I walk down the concrete path out of prison with
his mother, who starts to cry once we are out of sight. I try to
comfort her, but what do you say to a mother whose baby boy is
a convicted murderer serving life without parole?

She doesn't look frail but she feels feeble when I put my arm
around her as she cries. She straightens up and blows her nose in
a tissue as we wait in line to go through the gates. I walk with her
out to the parking lot where Stella is waiting to take her home.
We say our good-byes in the light rain outside of Stella's un-
opened car. Since it's obvious that Mrs. Polizzi isn't going to introduce me to Stella, whom I can barely see inside, I wish Tony's
mom a pleasant evening and walk to my car.

We all have our walls.

I spend the evening as I do on most of the visits, reading,

watching *Law & Order,* listening to the trucks drive by on 101
outside the walls of my Travelodge nest.

The next morning when I see Mrs. Polizzi, she seems almost
chipper. She tells me that she won a little money last night playing blackjack at a casino just out of town. I note that she doesn't
share any details about the evening, which I assume she'd spent
with Stella. She's friendly but reserved. I say how Tony is so
proud of his Italian heritage and is always reminding Rory that
his Irish beauty is really half Italian.

"I'm Irish, too," says Tony's mother. And I can't wait to go inside and divulge that bit of news to Rory.

Our second visiting day passes much as the first did, with
Rory and Tony bantering, bickering. Rory's thrilled when I tell
him about Tony's mom being Irish. He teases Tony about it
when they wait on line near the vending machines during the
first bathroom break at 11:00 a.m. Tony's ticked off we found
out and insists his mother is only half Irish, which makes him
mostly Italian and not a liar.

In an effort to regain his pride, Tony barks at us that we'd
better get some food out of the machines before it's all gone.
Rory and I aren't hungry. We spend most of the day oblivious to
everyone else and lost in each other.

Rory calls our visiting days "years disguised as hours."

Safe in the cocoon of our love's creation, we bare ourselves
and that casts a healing light on our wounds. Before everything
went wrong for Rory, before his mother found God and the
minister molested him, he remembers some happy times and
how she tried to give them some semblance of a normal childhood. At Christmastime, she'd instruct Rory and his little sister
to gather their stuffed animals and dolls, and then the three of
them would construct a unique nativity scene in the living

room. He remembers "Cabbage Patch Jesus," swaddled in a blue towel, always at the center of their mismatched tableau. At their father's house they'd get expensive toys and games, but that's not what Rory thinks about when he thinks of Christmas. It's Cabbage Patch Jesus. He says that if we had a life together in the real world he'd want to do that with our children, create a Cabbage Patch Christmas.

"Or maybe we could use Frankie Bear," I suggest, referring to the stuffed animal I've had since I was a kid and still sleep with. I first told him about Frankie in a letter in the early days when Rory was asking me mundane details about my life, trying to picture me in my home. He loved this silly news because Francis is Rory's middle name. It's one of the first coincidences he read as evidence of a deep connection between us.

It was Christmas that really brought Rory and me together, a year ago, when I bared my pain about not having my own family. I tell him how my mother thinks I am getting better with all of that, but I admit that it still hurts to see everyone else in my family with their kids.

"My mother is mad at Alexei," I tell Rory.

"You should be, too."

But how do you get mad at someone who was molested as a child and confused sexually as an adult? Very early on after the divorce, I asked Alexei if he thought he was always gay and if the sexual abuse by men disgusted him so much that he denied his own identity. He said he could never know the answer to that question. He told me that he thought of our nearly nine years together as the happiest in his life. I shouldn't hold on to his crumbs, but I do.

"He didn't mean for this to happen," I tell Rory.

"He lied to you," he says. No one, no therapist, no friend, no sibling, had ever said it so bluntly like that. Or maybe I wouldn't let them say it. Here, safe with Rory, I finally hear the truth. Alexei lied, whether he meant to or not.

Rory asks me why I am so understanding of other people's pain but always brush my own aside. In this year of clarity Rory has given me, I tell him I hope to be able to answer that question so that I can finally move on. I have had this conversation with other people—my mom, my brothers, my friends—but Rory doesn't look at me with eyes that say he wished he knew how to ease my pain. His eyes do not convey empathy; they contain the knowledge of holding my pain inside his own heart.

"Clarity" his eyes silently pray for me. As he brushes my cheek with one hand and slowly strokes my velvet-covered arm up and down with his other one, our breathing meshes. I passed through the thresholds of nine rainbows to get to this gaze, where I see no worry, only the confidence that I will find what I need from within.

"Restroom break," the corrections officer sitting on the platform says into the PA system, breaking our spell. I ask Rory if he wants to go and he says he needs to relax first. "My queen doesn't know what effect she has on her subject," he says, with his crooked grin. He wants me to look down at the bulge in his pants. "When you look at me wide open like that, I want you more than any other woman in the world," he says, sitting up straight, pulling his legs under the table, and tapping his feet on the ground. "But I can't think of that now."

When Rory comes back from the restroom I think it best that I reiterate how, even though I love him, I cannot stay in this dream world with him forever. He knows, he says, adding that he'd never let me do his time. I wonder about these other women—how they cope, why they keep coming back. A good percentage of the couples I've seen in this visiting room consist of a younger inmate and an older, often heavy-set, woman. I ask Rory what he thinks is going on with some of them.

"Do I think some of these guys are just romancing them for the visits, or money, or things they might send? Yeah," he says. He looks at one such couple walking around in a counterclock-wise circle outside on the patio. "But we don't know what's going on," he continues, in a tone I recognize as his loving "you don't know everything, Bridget" voice. "She's getting something out of it, too." As for her weight, Rory points out that perhaps her wounds have found a more obvious physical way of showing than mine, manifested in shaking hands.

We tend to fall in love with people who possess the exact qualities we need to work on in ourselves. Sitting there with Rory steadying my hands, I admit I can be quick to judge. Maybe that's why I cannot meet someone on the outside, I spec-ulate. "Sometimes I think I should just find a good-enough guy and settle," I say. It is a throw-away line, which I didn't even re-ally think about before saying, but ten days later when Rory's post-visit letter arrives, it is very much on his mind:

> But Bridget! You are so much more special than that, than all of the others who have given up and settled for less. You were not meant for a pretend love and its numb plati-tudes. For over time that is a whole different kind of sorrow, I would think. To know. To look in the mirror and know that after so long, after being so strong, after all of the searching and struggling and pain to find true love . . . you gave up.
>
> I will not go on about this.

If you settle for comfort, Bridget, I will not think less of you. I could never love you less than now, only more. And I will forever be here for you, when you need me, when you crave what we share, what we both know is so special.

And I will try to explain to you why whatever you do, you will not hurt me more than I could bear. Simply because I know in my heart of hearts that what we have is true and could've, would've, been exactly what the whole world dreams of having. For it was not "taken" from us, only not given the chance of reality. No, our perfect love was never taken, therefore it will always and forever be there, true, waiting for a chance to be born in a reality of a different time.

Next time, I'll find you sooner.

Bridget, my love, to have the only hope that has ever really mattered to me . . . to see it come into reality in your smile, your words, your eyes . . . to finally know that it is not hope any longer, but rather a rare treasure that truly exists! . . . It makes my entire sad life okay somehow. Not my deeds, but my sorrow. And that is enough. For every wound carved upon my heart is now healed.

You make me feel braver than I really am. Brave enough to heal you. For the past is but a dream, sometimes good and sometimes bad, but must be forgotten to live fully today. Because you truly do deserve to live fully, my love.

After visiting with Rory, and getting his post-visit letters, I always feel more connected with myself. When I meet my friend Karen for lunch on Valentine's Day, she says I'm glowing. I try to explain how it's not just the effect all the affection Rory pours on

me during our visits that is lifting me—it's my conscious transfer of my pain to his heart.

"He's locking it away," I tell her. I don't know why I spoke to
Rory of settling for a good-enough guy, I explain, because what
I really need to settle has nothing to do with finding a partner in
life. I know I need to deal with the kid thing once and for all, and
Rory's love strengthens me as I try to let go.

The news of the day that San Francisco's mayor, Gavin New-
som, is allowing gay marriages in City Hall does not even make
me feel bitter about Alexei.

"I think that shows growth," I tell Karen.

Karen put aside her dreams of having children when she
married an older man who already had children. Women who
marry prisoners are not the only ones who accept limitations in
favor of a union with someone they love. I am one of the few
people Karen talks with about how she is grappling with not
having kids now that she is thirty-six. She loves her husband,
and I have seen how happy they are together, but she understands the pangs that come with not having children.

"I like Rich's kids a lot, but they are not mine," she says over
a Caesar salad and a glass of chardonnay.

"It's okay to be sad about it," I say over my identical lunch.
"The thing that gets me is that in this baby-obsessed world,
those of us who grieve not having children are supposed to just
shut up, or else we sound like we're whining." I don't want to
whine about it, I just want to be understood. "Rory's helping me
with that. For the first time in years, I am thinking in hopeful
ways about the future—even if I don't know what it's going to
be." I tell Karen that I don't even feel sad about not having someone to spend Valentine's Day with because Rory sent me a card
with a story of our fantasy life in it.

"I know it's weird," I say, "but playing out this fantasy with Rory is starting to block out the sadness I feel when I think about all that I had and lost with Alexei." It's like what Rory said in his letter: our life together may not be real, but it also was never snatched away. I think that's what I never got over with Alexei: how just when it seemed I had everything I'd wanted, he disappeared.

"What does Rory do for you that a therapist couldn't?" she asks.

"He loves me." It's as simple as that.

After lunch, Karen suggests we check out the little shop where we found the cocktail dress that she got the other ladies to buy for my fortieth birthday. I think about buying a cute cloche hat until I try on a pair of pink corduroy pants that Karen says make my butt look great. "I know Rory's going to love that," I say. She pays for a purse she found while I get changed. I buy the cords.

When we get outside she takes the hat from her bag and hands it to me.

"Happy Valentine's Day," she says. I want to protest, but I can see that giving me the hat makes her happy. I tell her that every time I wear it I'll remember this day, when a good friend understood how a real but fantasy relationship with a man in prison turned out to be the key to finally unlocking my past.

Every other month, I make the trip to see Rory. I fold our days together between the realities of my work and social life like precious pressed flowers. Most of our visits are the same—a lot of lovin' and time lost in healing dreams. But when Rory called at the end of June I heard something foreign in his voice: fear.

"They rolled Tony up," he says. He explains how the cops have been sweating on Tony and Stella, who had started to visit him after waiting to be approved for months. To the corrections officers Stella's a turncoat, since she went from working in the prison to being involved with an inmate.

"They trashed our cell when I was at work, and when I came back Tony was gone," continues Rory. He tried to send a kite— an illegal intraprison note—to Tony in the SHU, but he hasn't heard back. He doesn't want to say too much on the phone, because the COs are probably listening for Rory to divulge something about Tony and Stella's relationship.

"Five years with Tony in this cell is the most stability I've ever had in my life," he says. "That's pathetic, but true." His laughter sounds forced.

I want to offer comfort but I am not sure what to say. Rory says just hearing my voice is helping to bring his pulse down. If Tony's going to be in the SHU for any length of time, Rory says he will try to find a new celly before the prison assigns him someone he doesn't want to live with.

Our alloted fifteen minutes speeds by. After I hear the mechanical voice give us the one-minute warning, I blurt out that I'll try to come and see him on the weekend. We get disconnected as we say "I love you" at the same time.

He didn't ask me to come, he would never ask me to do anything that would interrupt my life, but I think Rory knew I'd make the trip.

I get to the prison so early on Saturday that I am there even before Ruth, who is usually the first one at Pelican Bay on visiting days. They open the processing center at 8:30 and usually accommodate the SHU visitors first, but since my paperwork went through with theirs, it's only 8:45 when I am called and cleared. Ruth is right behind me.

The door into the visiting room is unlocked and unguarded. It takes a few minutes for one of the four guards hanging around the platform inside to notice us. A female guard I haven't seen before takes our IDs and tells us to "go on in," like we are here for a party. The door the prisoners use to come in and out of is open, too, and I peek inside to see what their processing area looks like. It's an empty corridor intersection painted an institutional tan with a bare desk against the right side wall and what looks the side of a cage around one corner.

The guard at the desk on the platform is one of the regulars. "I think this is the earliest I've ever been here," I say as I give him my pass. He assigns me a table near the vending machines and I ask if we might sit near the windows instead. He's nice enough to grant my request. He possesses a power not unlike a maître d', except the racial tensions among the prison population and gang affiliations present unusual seating challenges. He knows "Mehan" is going to be okay wherever he seats us, because Rory's got a good rep for getting along.

Rory looks different when he comes out, but I can't place what's changed. Maybe he is more frightened than he had let on on the phone. He hugs me gently and kisses me in the smooth, familiar way we do in the mornings, without any trace of hunger or neediness.

When we sit down and take each other's hands, he tells me he is wearing Tony's clothes. That's what's odd. And it dawns on me that I've seen Rory in the same exact jeans and blue shirt for a year now. "Tony's not going to be needin' his blues any time soon," says Rory.

In the five days since his phone call, he's tried to piece together why Tony got rolled up. He also asked me to call Stella and Tony's mother, and so we compare notes. Rory thinks the COs are trying to prove that something happened between Tony and Stella while she still worked as free staff in the laundry. All she told me is that since she started visiting Tony everyone she knew in town turned against her. The women she used to play cards with stopped inviting her, and the COs hassled her whenever she visited Tony, making her change her clothes a few times or interrupting their visits, saying they were sitting too close.

Tony's mother didn't know anything. When I called her all she said was "well, that's a nice birthday present," because Tony's birthday was a few days away. She had her plane ticket and was planning to visit in a couple of weeks, but now she'd have to cancel her plans. I gave her my number and asked her to call me if she heard anything, but she didn't call.

"They're talking about transferring him," says Rory. "Man, I miss 'im."

As if having his celly rolled up wasn't enough, Rory tells me about what happened the week before that almost landed him in the hole. Rory never needs to search for words, but he struggles with how to explain what he couldn't talk about on the phone. He saw two white guys go into the shower with shanks. Rory stayed on the other side of the bathroom wall, near the sinks, but he heard them jump a black inmate and then the guards came rushing in. They took the stabbed inmate to the infirmary and were about to throw Rory into the SHU with the two other white inmates when a CO piped up that "Mehan" didn't have anything to do with it.

Rory sits hunched over the table concentrating on our hands, stroking my fingers with his as he recounts the event.

I ask if they killed the black inmate. "Nah, they stuck him good, and there was lots of blood. I don't think they wanted to kill him. . . ." He looks past my shoulder before he continues. "I've seen worse stuff than that in here over the years." He turns to look at me. "But now that I feel human again . . . it's just different."

"And a week later Tony's gone. No wonder you feel shaken," I say. "I thought shaking was my thing." My comment eases Rory and he sits back in his chair and watches Pamela come through the door.

He says Pete's on him to cell-up together. I don't think that is such a good idea, I say. "He's a slob, but he's okay," Rory says. Still, he thinks he might ask another younger guy on the tier to move in with him while Tony's gone. He's been talking with the guy all week, checking him out. Rory needs to move someone in before the prison rooms him with a child molester or worse.

"A murderer?" I ask.

"Some of my best friends are murderers," he jokes.

"Yeah, mine too. Thanks."

Rory cracks a smile and moves his chair closer to mine. He says the problem with the young inmate is that he's seventeen and a newbie, so he doesn't know the routine yet. Rory shakes his head and says, "It looks like I'm gonna raise a kid in prison."

At thirty-one, Rory's not exactly an old-timer, but he's a seasoned enough inmate to take a kid under his wing. He might even move the kid in that night, if the kid agrees.

Just then the guard from the platform comes over to us and tells "Mehan" to move his chair to the opposite side of the table. He's nice about it, but says they've changed the rules and our chairs have to be on opposite sides of the table and not next to each other. We comply. They're always tweaking the visiting room rules. Later, when we go to the vending machines to get juice and a couple of frozen breakfast burritos, Pete points out the taped quadrangle parameter on the floor in front of the machines, which inmates are now supposed to stay behind. The signs posted say that any inmate caught shaking the machines to dislodge a stuck item will have his visit terminated.

"They hate us," is what Rory usually says about all the ways the system imposes itself on them so they never forget who, and what, and where they are. One time, when an alarm went off inside, they made all of the inmates in the visiting room sit on the floor. I held Rory's hand as he sat there, but I knew he was embarrassed. I felt bad for the guys humiliated in front of their children like that.

It's all part of life on what Rory calls "the prison planet."

He worries it will get the best of him. His biggest fear is that he'll forget there is a real world beyond his thirteen-inch television screen, as he has watched so many other lifers do. It's why he thinks the distraction of a young celly might help him. It's why he loves to write so much, to inhabit a world outside the bars.

The one good thing about having the cell to himself, he says, is that he's been able to work on several books at once. He calls it "multitasking worlds." He has one idea he likes more than the others and he wants to tell me about it. It's based on his life.

As a teenager, Rory once broke into an apartment when he was between living arrangements. At first he'd sneak in only to sleep at night, but eventually he started living there and snooping around. He says the place was set up as if the guy who lived there stepped out for milk or something, but he had been gone for nine years. "Somebody was payin' his bills," he says. "I ran up a huge electric bill and someone paid it without even coming around to check it out. Who does that?"

While he was living there, Rory used to dream that the guy's brother would come by and he'd hide in the crawl space above the ceiling and watch the guy wash his dishes. The guy would say to the air, "There's a reason my brother's missing, and if you don't watch out, the same could happen to you."

I ask how long he stayed in that apartment. Rory smiles his crooked smile and says, "I wound up sleeping with the neighbor and getting into a fight with her husband." Typical Rory, I think. He ran away when the husband called the police.

He tells me that in the story he's writing about it, he'll make me the neighbor. He's very pleased with that idea.

The missing guy's name was Tom McGraw, and Rory thinks that if he can solve the mystery of Tom McGraw's life on the page, it might illuminate some of the mysteries he is still trying to solve in his own. Then he tries out his opening line on me:

"What we fear the most in life never reaches us, but rather, it is what we love that destroys us in the end."

He scrunches his nose. He knows it's not quite right.

It's a good opening line, but we both know that when love is pure and equally given it is the only healing balm. It's why I ran up to see him when he needed me. It's what he gives me in every letter. Without it, I might not have found hope again through him and he might not have felt human again through me.

Love truly shared leads to freedom, one of those intangible things lurking under a rainbow. The trick is recognizing which rainbow holds your pot of gold.

CHAPTER 10

NAOMI

To tell or not to tell—that is ultimately the question for each of the women at Pelican Bay as I approach them about sharing their stories. Naomi was one of the first to say yes, and her cousin, Laurie, was one of the first to say no.

Not that Laurie is unfriendly toward me—in fact, she is just the opposite. It's just that her husband would prefer that she not share anything personal about their relationship with me and I can respect that.

Naomi and Laurie live on a Native American reservation outside of Eureka, where they grew up together. They are both in their midforties; Naomi is a year older and, at five feet tall, an inch or two shorter than her younger cousin. They both wear their dark hair straight just below their shoulders. With their matching round faces, high cheekbones, and bright dark eyes, they could be sisters. They like to say that they think of themselves that way. They both talk about watching their weight, but neither of them can be bigger than a size six. What I notice most about Naomi and Laurie is how they radiate an enormous sense of generosity and hospitality.

Both of them had extended open invitations for me to stay

with them at their homes on the reservation, but since Naomi is the one willing to go on the record, I decide to take her up on the offer first. She's thrilled when I tell her I am coming, because that August weekend happens to coincide with her tribe's annual heritage celebration. She describes it as a carnival, with games, music, lots of Native American (although she says "Indian") food, and even a rodeo.

The only time I remember being on an Indian reservation was when we visited my uncle Bill's family in Colorado after they moved there in the 1970s. Snapshots of my cousins and siblings poking their heads through teepees (probably set up for us tourists) float through my mind as I make my way up and around two summits in the forested mountains outside of Eureka. I remember my dad and his brother Bill having some fun with us—eleven Kinsellas packed in a rented station wagon—as we came down from Pikes Peak. "I don't know about these brakes, Bill," my father said, planting the seed for their ruse. By the time we were halfway down the mountain my big brothers had convinced me and my two younger cousins that each turn on the winding road put us in utter peril, transforming a family outing into a squealing roller-coaster ride.

From what Naomi's told me about her life on the reservation, I expect to land in a setting where extended families live and tease much like my own.

When I call Naomi from the road at about 5:30 p.m., she says she is running late. She is just finishing up her work at the office of a family wellness organization where she assists caseworkers who help people dealing with alcohol and drug addiction. Since it will take her about an hour to get home, and she also has to pick up her grandchildren from day care, she suggests I call Laurie and go hang out with her for a while.

Laurie seems delighted to hear from me and tells me to come right over. I pull off to the side of the road and scribble down her complicated directions. Being the city/suburban girl that I am, I get lost pretty quickly. I missed the turn-off on the freeway after the modest Baptist church Laurie used as a landmark in her directions. I know something is wrong when I pass a small high school and a motel that Laurie never mentioned. So I call her and she drives out to meet me. As I follow her home, I think that the reservation looks much like any rural California community, with mostly ranch houses tucked away off the side of back roads with names like Elk Creek Drive or Bear Claw Lane.

Laurie lives in a pristine, gray-painted double-wide on her parents' property just fifty yards from their yellow ranch house. We park our cars in her yard and make our way to the back of her parents' house, where Laurie's mother, niece, and her niece's four-year-old daughter are picking apples. Her twenty-something niece, Michelle, is going to use the apples to bake a couple of pies for the celebration that begins tomorrow morning.

"Michelle's the baker in the family," says Laurie.

Laurie's mother hands me an apple and its crisp, tart taste is a welcome refreshment on a hot day that is just starting to give way to a cool evening.

Laurie takes me to her house, where we sit on her back deck drinking iced tea. She recently moved back to the reservation and is clearly happy to be with her family. I already know she has been married to Kevin for more than a decade and does not have any children. "Someone's always coming around," she says as Annie, the four-year-old, climbs onto the deck to join us. Annie stands behind an exercise bicycle and eyes me, while Laurie and I talk. When Laurie goes inside to answer the phone, Annie follows her and comes back out with a puzzle of Moses and the Ten Commandments that she wants me to help her put together. When we finish, she goes in and gets another puzzle, and this time she easily leans against my bare legs as I try to teach her the trick about finding the end pieces first.

When Laurie comes out again she tells Annie to let us have some visiting time. The girl squirms through the deck's gate, without opening it fully, and heads over to play with her great-grandmother's small dog in the yard. But she's back on the deck in no time asking me to do another puzzle. "Oh, Anners," says Laurie.

She suggests we all go to her mother's house and see how Annie's mother's pies are coming along.

Out of respect for Laurie, whose husband doesn't want her to share anything too private in writing, I cannot say much about my visit with her family except that they make me feel completely welcome, which is a good thing, because Naomi doesn't show up until after 9:30 p.m. She walks in through the open kitchen door of her aunt's house without knocking, with her three-year-old granddaughter, Paige, and eight-year-old grandson Bobby in tow. As happens in families who see each other regularly, no one embraces hello. Naomi settles down on one of three couches in the living room, all pointed at a big-screen TV. Annie takes Paige off to play in one of the bedrooms and Bobby takes his Game Boy out of his knapsack and sits down near his grandmother.

The news anchor on the big-screen TV is going on about another change in airport security and Michelle shares an incident that occurred with her friends at the Los Angeles airport. "A whole bunch of security guards came rushing at us. And, yeah, we're Indian, so we put our hands up," she says. "Then they ran right past us." Everyone else laughs at the image, but I'm thinking about how, as a white woman, I'd never think the cops were coming toward me. My instinct would be to look behind me to see what was going on.

It strikes me how, as much we are the same, we are different. Even my darkest Italian relatives will never know what it is like to internalize society's suspicion based on the color of her skin. Until that moment, I don't think I really understood on something deeper than an intellectual level that there are things about race that I just cannot fathom. It's a good lesson and I am grateful to Naomi and her family for it, but I don't articulate the point. They have already moved on to the topic of forest fires, anyway, because Naomi's daughter is away at her job bringing supplies to firefighters working on a blaze about an hour away.

The time ticks by and I think that one thing my family does share with this one is how long it takes to say good-bye—even without the hugs. It's after eleven when we leave.

I follow Naomi toward her home through windy redwood- and pine-tree-lined roads. Over my right shoulder I catch a glimpse of the stark, full moon against a pitch-black night sky, and my eyes marvel at a contrast I've seldom seen. The moon appears to be resting on the very side of the mountain.

Naomi's four-bedroom ranch sits on top of a hill. Her sons, eighteen and nineteen, are out and the house is dark. It's a little late for a house tour, so she shows me to the master bedroom, which her daughter usually shares with Paige. The smell of disinfectant wafts out of the attached bathroom, and I realize that after work and picking up her grandkids, Naomi spent much of the evening cleaning for my sake. She gives me a towel and we say good night.

Lying in Naomi's daughter's bed, I hear music coming up from their nearest neighbor at the bottom of the hill. Paige is screaming from Naomi's bedroom down the hall. She quiets down about midnight, which is when Naomi's sons come home. They put the television on in the living room and the phone rings a few times until about 1:30 in the morning. Rather than being bothered by the nighttime cacophony, I smile as I roll over on my side smelling fabric softener on the sheets, thinking that these are the sounds of several generations living under one roof.

I wake up early but stay in bed until I hear some movement in the house. I find Naomi alone in the kitchen making coffee for us. She's in the middle of redecorating and the furniture in her dining/living rooms rests on bare, unfinished floorboards. Naomi says she is getting new carpeting this week. The living room furniture consists of a couple of couches and a cushy chair arranged around a square coffee table and a big-screen TV. A blanket with a large image of the risen Christ lines the back of the couch I sit on.

Having grown up in a Catholic home, the display of religious iconography always comforts me, but I can imagine how a non-Christian might find it odd or even unsettling. We had our own special statue of the Virgin Mary. When my sister Claire was in the second grade, St. Ann's was getting new statues of the Virgin for all the classrooms and Claire asked if she could bring one of the old Marys home for her mother. I don't know how she managed to walk the quarter mile to our house carrying a three-dimensional replica of Mary that was nearly her own size, but Claire's herculean effort made my mother treasure her gift even more. That's how Mary on the mantel, in huge disproportion to picture frames and other knickknacks kept there, came to be what anyone entering our home noticed first.

So, Naomi's got Jesus on her couch. She says she likes to start her days sipping coffee in her living room, watching one of the televangelist shows she has on her TiVo. This morning it's T. D. Jakes and his "Ten Commandments of Working in a Hostile Environment." He's talking about how God sometimes reaches out through people we find difficult.

Naomi asks if Paige's screams kept me up. I lie. Her sons are already up and out. Naomi took the day off from work, but she plans to drop Paige off at day care anyway, so that we can have some peaceful time at the tribal festivities.

"Do they live here with you all the time?" I ask about Paige and Bobby.

"Yeah, my daughter comes and goes depending on her work," says Naomi. Her daughter is twenty-eight and is not married to the father of her daughter, who lives elsewhere on the reservation. Naomi doesn't mention anything about her grandson's father. Naomi had her daughter when she was just eighteen and, even though she didn't marry her daughter's father, she stayed with him for ten years. She had her boys with another man she didn't marry. Her relationship with Daniel, who is serving twenty-five to life at Pelican Bay, is her first marriage.

I ask Naomi what her children think of her relationship with Daniel. She says that her daughter hasn't met him and thinks her mom might have bumped her head, but she doesn't say much more about it. Her boys have both met Daniel, but Naomi adds that with him serving life, they don't think he'll ever come live there. "So it's safe for them," she says. "And they see how happy I am."

I think about going to get my tape recorder, but then Bobby comes into the living room and pops in a DVD of the movie *Rush Hour*, ending Naomi's quiet time.

"We should get ready anyway," she says.

The weather report calls for sunny skies and temperatures in the nineties, so I wear a skirt, tank top, sneakers, and baseball cap. Then I lather up my skin with sunscreen (SPF 50), before heading out the door with Naomi and her grandchildren. Bobby sits in the back of the car with his iPod and Paige keeps trying to get out of the car as Naomi runs back and forth from the house fetching things for the day's outing. I notice that Naomi's "prison purse" sits between the two front seats.

Whereas I still use a Ziploc bag to bring my money and keys into prison, the wives, mothers, and steady girlfriends of inmates usually have purchased some kind of more permanent clear plastic purse. I guess Naomi uses hers all the time.

When she finally gets in the car and we start down her driveway, Naomi points out the prickly brambles all along the side of her yard and says, "My husband's got a lot of work to do when he comes home."

Even though Daniel's got twenty-five to life, Naomi says they believe God will bring him home to her. And, I think, to a ranch house on a hill on an Indian reservation he has never seen. I ask Naomi about Daniel's background and she says he's "Caucasian." I laugh and try to explain how, even though it is the box I check off without thinking on every form I fill out, the word sounds strange to me spoken out loud and I would never use it to describe myself. Then she tells me Daniel's Jewish, which makes me think how many Jewish people do not consider themselves white, and yet they tick off the Caucasian box, too.

"Huh," she says, "I never thought of that."

Naomi has told me that Daniel was a gang member in Los Angeles, where he grew up and lived in a series of foster homes. He's been in and out of prison since his early twenties, although she has never been specific about his crimes. All she offers is that he landed at Pelican Bay eight years ago, when he got twenty-five to life because of California's three-strikes law. She met Daniel through Laurie and her husband, Kevin, whom he knew through the Christian ministry in prison.

I am dying to ask a barrage of questions, but with the kids in the backseat and the day's activities ahead, I know I will not be able to record or take notes. So I decide to just enjoy the day.

When we arrive at the Tribal Community Center, which looks like any community center built in America after the 1970s, I think the atmosphere is more like a small-town fair than a carnival, as Naomi had described. There are booths with food, T-shirts, and handmade jewelry. At 10:30 a.m., there are already hundreds of people milling about. Naomi's grandson wants to try the rock climbing wall and the electric bull ride. All the activities are free, and we lose sight of Bobby for more than an hour. We run into Laurie, who has her mother's tiny dog on a leash, and we go sit under a tent in front of the central stage.

An announcer introduces young girls wearing native dress as they parade across the stage. He points out that some of the girls appear in clothes worn by their great-grandmothers. Later on the stage there are pie-eating contests and even something called "Native American Idol." One girl who looks about twelve is so nervous that she turns her back on the crowd before singing her tryout song. Much like its TV equivalent, most of the songs come from American top-forty radio.

It's clear that Naomi is well liked by the warm way people greet her as we walk around. But one man, who is obviously strung out on something, comes up to Naomi and says, "I got my J number," which means a prison number and that he is an ex-con. I wonder if he is approaching her because of her work with addicts or because he knows about her husband. Naomi calmly says, "That's good. We'll see you down at church, right?"

Naomi spots her sons, who are with her ex-boyfriend. "Daniel doesn't like when he comes around," she says about her ex. "But my boys like him." She briefly introduces me to them, but we quickly move on.

Naomi insists that I try my first Indian taco, which is really a mound of beans, rice, onions, tomatoes, and sour cream piled on top of a piece of Indian fry bread. It's not for the calorie-conscious connoisseur, but it's messy, delicious, and very filling. There's a rodeo and live music planned for that night, and Naomi asks me to stay, but I want to move on to Crescent City and to my Travelodge so that I can be fresh for visiting Rory the next morning.

At one point on my winding drive over two summits, I get stuck behind a hay truck—a reminder of the peek I'd just had at a rural life I've never known. Two mountains might separate Naomi and Daniel, but all of us who know people in prison live in a world they cannot really know. At best, we can bring our outside lives in through our pictures and stories.

But Rory says that beats watching TV, any day.

Rory and I are already sitting at a table in the back of the visiting room the next day when Naomi and Laurie arrive at 10:00 a.m. The guard assigns Naomi to a table next to us and Laurie to one across the room. Laurie comes to hang out with Naomi at her table as they wait for their guys to come out, and I thank them for showing me such a good time.

"I had my first Indian taco," I boast to Rory.

"Yeah, with the fry bread?" he asks.

The four of us enjoy some illegal cross-visiting, until Laurie stiffens up at the sight of her husband coming through the prison door. She hastens back to her table. Rory and I go outside and sit at a concrete picnic table. We sit next to each other holding our hands on top, but within a few minutes a guard comes over and tells us that Rory can't sit next to me. Usually I've noticed that when a guard interrupts a visit, he addresses himself solely to the inmate. But this corrections officer is one that Rory likes, and after he tells him to move, the guard looks at me and says, "I'm sorry."

"It's the rules," I say with a shrug.

When the officer leaves us alone, Rory starts to laugh. He explains that every time he sees this CO, who's tall, built, and has a shaved head and a baby face, he pictures him in buttless chaps at the Blue Oyster, a gay bar that figures prominently in all of the *Police Academy* movies. Rory hums the opening notes of the Blue Oyster theme song, but having never seen a *Police Academy* movie in my life, I have no idea what he's talking about.

"You're in love with a silly man," he says.

When Laurie and Kevin come out to walk around the patio, I ask Rory what he thinks of him. "I don't like the way he talks about his wife," he says. Apparently Kevin is not happy that Laurie moved back to the reservation. "She's with her people being independent Laurie and she doesn't need him so much." Rory says Kevin does not want Laurie to associate much with women connected to the prison, even Naomi.

"But they're cousins," I say.

"Look, he's already on her," he says. Laurie is in a corner of the patio with her back against the wall and Kevin, who is tall and bulky, stands with his hands on his hips towering above her. Rory suggests that I not say too much to Kevin about my visit to the reservation. Apparently, Kevin is also not that keen about my hanging out with Laurie because I'm not Christian.

"I dare him to say that to my face," I say. It bothers me when people use religion to divide themselves from others. Rory agrees with me, but he says some evangelical Christians would not acknowledge my faith as Christian. And, he says, some Catholics are not that open-minded, either. After he was arrested and found guilty of murder, he called his Catholic grandparents and they offered to send a priest to meet with Rory. "When I told them that we weren't Catholic anymore but joined a Christian church, they hung up," says Rory. "The murder they could deal with, but not being Catholic, that was unforgivable."

I let it go because, to me, this all seems ludicrous.

I ask Rory what he thinks of Daniel and Naomi.

"I know he loves her, and I hope she's happy," says Rory. "But he's also got her convinced that God will let him out of here, when he's got life." One time, Rory continues, Daniel had Naomi so convinced that he was coming home on a certain date that she prepared a homecoming feast for him complete with a "welcome home" banner. When Rory sees my skeptical look, he adds, "I saw the pictures of her with the banner."

I feel bad talking about Naomi like this.

"It's none of our business," says Rory. "I just don't like it when these guys lie about their time."

I make a mental note that I want to find out from Naomi if Daniel has life or twenty-five to life, and how that affects his ever coming home.

The visiting hours pass like they usually do: people heating up frozen food in the microwave and eating it at their island tables.

At one point, I hear murmuring coming from Naomi and Daniel's table, with an audible "Jesus" or "Lord" intermittently thrust out from one or the other. They sit with their eyes shut, clasping hands.

"What was that?" I ask, as Rory and I walk outside. He tells me they were speaking in tongues.

I fight the urge to laugh. "Really?" I ask.

Rory says he tries not to judge anyone's religious practices. "But I've heard him go from 'Jesus' to 'ooooh-baby' in that same voice—and that creeps me out," says Rory, shaking his head.

"God and sex," I say, remembering how I pegged the two forces hovering over the visiting room from the very beginning. Rory and I do not pray together but God comes up a lot in conversation, but then so does Nietzsche, Buddha, Jung, and Freud (or as Rory likes to call him, Fraud).

We sit at a picnic table and I watch Naomi and Daniel inside with their eyes still closed, their lips moving. Rory says how everyone, everywhere is trying to find meaning in their lives.

We did it through loving each other. I remind him how we've been known to get lost in our dream world for hours—especially when I first started coming to visit. "I used to get hassled about it," says Rory. "They'd say, 'My girl's asking me, how come *you* don't look at *me* like *that?*'"

Even though their speaking in tongues strikes me as odd, on some level I understand how Naomi and Daniel connect to each other that way. When I was married, even though Alexei was baptized Lutheran, we enjoyed going to Sunday Mass together. Sharing the ritual of weekly Mass, where we'd kiss when it came time for giving each other a sign of peace, always made me feel more connected to my husband.

I know God is going to come up a lot when Naomi and I

sit down for the interview, and I want to keep an open mind about it.

"Is this like a testimony?" Naomi asks before we start the interview. We went out for coffee and now we sit in her car as it showers outside.

"A testimony?" I say, asking her to explain what she means. I take my tape recorder out of my purse.

At her prayer groups, she says, people often give brief testimonies about their lives before they actually pray.

I tell her that I will ask questions and that we'll just talk. Despite being one of the first who wanted me to interview her about her life with an inmate, Naomi tenses up immediately as I start to roll tape.

"Just tell me about your husband. You met him through your cousin who was married to an inmate. What did you think when your cousin married him?" I ask.

"I had a brother in prison," she says. "He died." The journalist in me wants to explore that, but with a reluctant subject, I sit back and let her speak.

"As for my cousin, I thought it was a little strange or weird that she'd go that way." Naomi leans against the driver's side door and sips her coffee. "Since it makes her happy, I support her." She sips again. "I always thought it was kind of one-sided, though. She's doing it all by herself out here with him in there. . . . It's unique."

"Then, lo and behold . . . ," I say, in a teasing, nonaccusatory way, trying to help Naomi relax.

"In all my dreams, I never guessed that I'd be involved with somebody in prison." She repeats how her first relationship lasted ten years and that she had her boys with another man, but she doesn't provide any specific details about either of them.

"Both of my children's fathers are deceased now," she says.

"Did they die when you were still with them?" I ask.

"No," she says flatly. "One died in a car wreck and the other . . . it, um . . . it was a tragedy that he was killed."

"Murdered?" I ask.

"Yeah, murdered," she says. "We were separated at the time, but still my boys were small and it was traumatic."

Again, the journalist side of my brain begs me to press her, but Naomi's shoulders are hunched and she looks as if she wants to melt into the car door behind her. I know she'll retreat. As much as I want to know about this part of her life, I am here to find out what led her to Daniel.

"I forgot we were recording, can I do it over?" asks Naomi. Yep, I think, she's having a hard time being open with me. So far three women who agreed readily to tell me their stories have either clammed up during the interview or changed their minds afterward.

"Don't worry," I say. "Just tell me what you want to. But the more you share, the more complete of a picture I can show. People always wonder why someone gets involved with an inmate. . . ."

"I guess to them it would be crazy. It's just not natural," says Naomi. But, when her cousin suggested she meet Daniel, Naomi was in an eight-year dead-end relationship. "He wanted children and I didn't," she says. So, as with everything in her life, Naomi took this problem to God. "I went on a five-day fast and on the fifth day my husband wrote to me." Laurie and Kevin had asked Daniel to write to Naomi, even though they had not met yet.

"I always wanted a man who was sold out for God and he wrote and told me he was Christian like I am," Naomi explains.

"Sold out for God?" I ask, but Naomi just says that means he sold out of everything else for God. I think it's an odd choice of words, but after she uses it over and over again, I figure that it's part of her jargon.

She continues with her story. "God sent me his letter over like a smoke signal. But, wouldn't you know it, he's locked up . . . and that was messed up." So Naomi put Daniel's letter aside and prayed for guidance. "I'm famous for getting myself into situations," she says, adding that most of the men she was involved with cheated on her.

Daniel asked Naomi to visit him and sent her money for gas.

"I wrote and told him that he better pour it on when I get there, because I got other guys out here and that might be my first and only visit," Naomi continues.

"Were you usually demanding like that with men?" I ask.

"No, never," she says. "And when I seen him, he looked different than his picture. We embraced as friends and we talked and we prayed." She says it was their prayer time that clinched it for her. "I thought that there really *are* men who love God the way I love God. And where I was living, I couldn't find that."

She says she and Daniel shared their stories on that first day. "He talked about being in prison and I talked about living on the reservation."

"How did you feel when he talked about his crime? You know, because your life has been touched by crime," I say.

Naomi hesitates and places her coffee in the cup holder between the car seats. "People ask me that . . . and if I have something for bad boys," she begins to answer, but then brings it back to God. "My whole thing is that I was looking for somebody who loved the Lord like I do. I never knew it would lead me to

Pelican Bay and to my husband. But it was totally all God that we met."

Then she blurts out that she actually asked Daniel to marry her. "It's funny, he said the words just came out of my mouth like we were playing a board game," says Naomi. It was sort of like playing Monopoly: she rolled the dice, passed Go, got her $200, and asked him to marry her three months after she first landed on Just Visiting.

"I came to see him every weekend. I couldn't get enough of him," she says. "We hugged on the first visit, and the second day we kissed. And that's pretty much how I met my husband."

I ask how Daniel courted Naomi.

"Just his attention. Men doing time in prison, you have 100 percent of their focus and you don't get that in the outside world," she says. "I see people out here are all distracted. My husband's focused—and that captivated me. His words are like honeycombs and I carry them around with me all week."

After they married four years ago, Naomi moved to Crescent City for two years to be with Daniel. Her youngest son was in high school, she says, and he wasn't too happy about the move. "He kept telling me that there were no Indians in school. And I told him they were watered-down tribes here," she explains. "But it was the best he'd ever done in school."

She's been back on the reservation for over a year now, but Naomi remembers her time in Crescent City as a vacation from her life.

"If I went out and left a pop in the fridge, it'd be there when I got back," she says. "And there'd be no messes to come home to. When you live with a big family there's always something."

"Was it a bit like living in a way station?" I ask.

"You live for those visits," she says. "The whole time I was here it was like a break, which is sort of what the visits are still like."

Naomi found the same kind of work in Crescent City that she had done before, helping addicts.

"Were you an addict yourself?" I ask. I know my question is going to put that deer-in-headlights look back on her face, but there is no way to avoid it. "Naomi," I start, "you talk quite a lot about being saved by God, and most people who talk about being saved so much usually have come out of something."

"You did," she says, wide-eyed. "You hit the nail on the head, there. God delivered me from addiction." And with this admission, Naomi appears at ease for the first time, taking the support of the car door that just minutes ago she appeared to be thrust up against as if held at gunpoint.

"I've had a lot of death in my life, including my mother. And they never found her," says Naomi. "It's been at least twenty-two years, and I never had any closure."

Naomi narrates the saddest story of her life without hardly blinking or changing the flat inflection in her voice.

Twenty-two years ago, Naomi was living with the father of her daughter and taking some classes at a community college. And she was partying pretty heavily, with booze and pot. One time, she was out with her mother and they were going to meet up with friends to party. But Naomi kept getting an ominous feeling about something she couldn't express. Her mother was going to drive back to the reservation that night and come back in the morning. "Something inside said, 'Tell her don't go,'" Naomi remembers. "And she said, 'Babe'—my mother always called me Babe—'don't worry about it.' And she held her hand up to wave good-bye, and I thought, 'This is the last time I am going to see her.' And it was."

They found her mother's purse along the river where her car went off the road. They never found her body. Naomi says she started using all kinds of drugs in her grief until she finally became addicted to methamphetamine. Then Naomi says her mother came to her in a dream and told her she had to get right with God—that she needed to clean out for her daughter's sake.

Naomi does not look like she wants to cry; instead, her eyes seem to be concentrated on something I cannot see. She reminds me of how my mother looked on that first Mother's Day after Grandma died. "Excuse me," my mom said flatly, trying to compose herself. "It's just that I lost my mother this year." Obviously, she didn't have to explain to us, her family, but there was something in the flat way she said it and in the look in her eyes that reminds me of Naomi right now. It's an emptiness that only children who have lost mothers who loved them well can share. I wonder if Naomi still reaches for the phone to call her mom, like my mother still does years after Grandma's passing.

"Naomi," I say gently, "I have found, with most of the women I have talked with who are involved with inmates, that if there's a common thread, it's that we were all wounded."

"Yeah?" she says. "You found that? I wonder how some of the women do it, because if I didn't have God in my life, I couldn't be with someone in prison."

"What do you think is the biggest misconception people have about these relationships?" I ask.

"They think you're stupid and there's something wrong with you," says Naomi.

As she reaches out to pick up her coffee, I spot something written in ink on the inside of her arm.

"It's scripture," she says. "I've never done that before." She jotted down Bible passages she had wanted to read with Daniel. Bibles are the only real reading material in the prison visiting room.

"Is it like a God cheat sheet?" I ask, which makes her laugh.

"Our marriage is Christ-centered," she says. "I've never taken communion so much since I met my husband." She explains that at least once during every visit they use crackers and juice from the vending machines and pray over them as an offering to God. This is their communion. When Daniel gets out—and Naomi will not even entertain the idea that Daniel is not coming home to her—she tells me she thinks they will travel around with their little communion kit to celebrate their faith together wherever they are.

"But doesn't he have life?" I ask.

"Well, that's what it looks like on his record," she says. "But I have strong faith that there's change coming around. God led me to him, and He doesn't do things halfway." She will not be dissuaded by anyone, she says, not even the prison chaplain, who told her her marriage would last five years at best. "He said that's how long these things last," says Naomi. "It's been four for us, and I've actually known my husband for five years."

"Don't you ever get frustrated, living on the outside without Daniel?" I ask.

"I take it to prayer and take care of things on my own until he comes home," she says. "My husband might not be with me in the physical sense right now, but he is with me in the spiritual sense, and I can live with that."

The last thing Naomi says to me before I get out of her car is how her relationship with God is a little like a drug. But, she adds, it's more like medicine than a narcotic.

CHAPTER 11

MOTHER'S DAY

This prison journey takes me to many unexpected places—emotionally, spiritually, and physically—but I never thought that I'd wake up one day seriously praying, for the first time since the third grade, "Oh, God, please don't make this mean I have to be a nun."

Not that there's anything wrong with being a nun, or that I had anything against them. After Rory's celly was sent to the SHU, I started to do some research on prison families and I met a couple of nuns at a conference I attended in October. The sisters ran a program called Get on the Bus that brings children into prisons on Mother's Day weekend to visit their incarcerated mothers. Once I knew about it, I couldn't look away.

When I called Sister Suzanne Jabro down in Los Angeles, who runs the Get on the Bus program, she was delighted to hear from me. "I knew you'd do something," she said. "Some people talk, and others do." Sister Suzanne, who asked me to call her simply Suzanne, is a doer. But I wasn't sure what exactly I wanted to "do" with these kids, I told her. I had just turned forty-one and I was still trying to put the pain of not having children of my own aside. Suzanne shared how she had found ways of mothering in her life as a nun that she had never expected. She grew up in a family of boys, and so the last thing she thought she'd do was live with a bunch of women. She used to work with men in prison, but now she is focused on the women and their children.

According to the U.S. Bureau of Justice, as of 2000, 1.5 million children in the United States have an incarcerated parent. That same study shows that women are being imprisoned at a more rapid rate than men; in the 1990s female prisoners rose by 106 percent and male prisoners by 58 percent. Suzanne told me that she worked with women in prison now because when men are incarcerated they are not usually the sole caretaker of their children, but the women are. Half of the children with mothers in prison live with their grandparents, who often do not have the means or the opportunity to bring their grandchildren to visit their mothers. Most prisons are in rural communities, whereas most of the children live in urban areas hours away. For some of the children the Mother's Day bus ride is the only time all year they will see their mothers.

I knew I was going to get on that bus come May, but in the meantime I needed to get over my own bitterness. And I knew I needed to see Rory—my support, my love—to talk this out.

At first he resists when I explain that I am laying to rest my dreams of having children. He wipes away my tears as I say it with a conviction I am just starting to own. And, as always, he speaks directly to my heart in his letter after the visit. He put pen to paper the next week, on Thanksgiving Day, watching the rain fall outside his sliver cell window:

My love for you is so much bigger and more important than my own broken dreams, and even before I got out of bed and saw the rain, I was smiling. For I let myself stay in my favorite place, that place that is in-between two worlds, aware of my wonderful dreaming and consciously able to nudge it ever so subtly, and I saw us both in a future filled with purpose and clarity, with happiness and love. And there was no regret over what could not be, for we were still connected and will always know that our love for each other is no less real because of it.

Do you know this now, too?

It was last weekend that solidified this truth inside of me, as I witnessed my beautiful angel rustle her mended wings, and there was quite suddenly the sensation of a great and powerful magic being proven true once and for all: The feeling that an epic journey through dark and treacherous times was very near its completion . . . And we were going to cross the finish line together, my love.

Of course, it did not start out that way.

What I saw in your eyes worried me, beautiful one.

But as you spoke, as you explained to me that you had taken one of the last three steps of this metamorphosis . . . Your trembling slowly evaporated from your bones, and that raw and painful look in your eyes gave way to that easy shining brilliance I so adore in you . . . And I realized it was only the proverbial "darkest hour" giving way to your amazing dawn . . .

. . . And didn't it feel like we kind of settled in nice and comfy together in this new stage of our relationship? It was as if we had known each other our entire lives . . . Like we

had been each other's first loves, and always will be, even though we'd taken separate paths somewhere along the way . . . And our love just simply is [underlined many times] . . . And it will forever be that way, no matter where we are or what we might be . . .

You are not the only one being healed.

Six months later, in May, I think of Rory as I stand on the steps outside of St. Leander church in San Leandro waiting to board a bus for two women's prisons located in Chowchilla, California. I see a sea of anxious kids' faces before me, and not a statistic among them.

Under cloudy skies at 7:30 a.m., the atmosphere in front of the church is celebratory. As it turns out, most of the people in the crowd are volunteers there to hand out donated Starbucks coffee and McDonald's Egg McMuffins, play music, and make the families of the incarcerated women feel like part of their community. When I find Jacqueline, the woman in charge of this particular bus, she tells me that only about twenty inmate families and a handful of volunteers will get on board. The rest, she says, are there for support because these kids often feel like outsiders wherever they go, just by having a mother in prison.

Jacqueline's husband gathers everyone, about seventy-five people, together in front of the church. He says that it doesn't matter what faith anyone is, all are welcome. Then he leads the group in singing "Amazing Grace." The church pastor speaks about how God guided Moses and Paul on their journeys and how He will guide us today. "They go as your blessing to their mothers to bring joy," he says. Then he evokes the scripture that includes, "For I was in prison and you visited me," which I recognize and complete in my mind, "Whatsoever you do, for the least of my brothers, that you do unto Me."

I can't help but smile as I get on board the bus and notice that ours (deemed the Oakland bus, even if we are leaving from neighboring San Leandro) is number 9—another of Rory's coincidences. He may be locked away, but he's nonetheless with me today. I take a seat and a seven-year-old Latino boy named Emanuel sitting in front of me with his auntie shows me that he is playing a game called "Duel" on his Game Boy. A baby in the back is crying but I have not met the others yet, so I don't know which family has brought along an infant. There are TV monitors on this moderately fancy bus but they are not switched on. Reese, the ten-year-old African American kid sitting across from me, says he wants to watch cartoons. He is eyeing Emanuel's Game Boy. They act like any other kids on a bus trip, except they are unusually quiet. We leave at 7:50 but turn back after ten minutes because someone called Jacqueline on her cell phone to tell her that one family showed up late. No one groans at the idea of going back; such grumbling would not suit the spirit of the day.

When the tardy family gets on board, Jacqueline looks relieved as she welcomes a grandmother named Lois and her granddaughter and two grandsons. Jacqueline says this is their third year on the bus.

Jacqueline fills us in on the day's itinerary and asks that a member of each family introduce the others in their group. The names of these kids blow me away. "Damien wants everyone to know to be on your best behavior," Jacqueline says for Damien, who is white, a little overweight, and looks about five. He is traveling with his grandmother. Skyler, a blond cherub with pale skin and green eyes set a little too far apart, looks to be about four and is traveling with her grandfather. When Jacqueline asks her to introduce her family member she says, "Papa." She asks Jacqueline when Mother's Day is again. "It's on Sunday," says Jacqueline. "This Friday is our special Mother's Day." This prompts Reese to my left to inquire, simply, "Can we go back on Sunday?"

His wish, which bestows a child's honest optimism, tugs at my heart as the introductions continue. I note that all of the children are on their best behavior—none of them needed to be told to sit quietly while others are speaking. Dylan, seven, is African American and with Grandma and Grandpa. Esmeralda, who looks like she is part black and Latina, introduces her grandmother. Jacqueline says Esmeralda's been riding the bus since the program started six years ago. Marisol speaks for the family we almost left behind. Jacqueline brags that Marisol's big brother, Javier, recently joined the Merchant Marines. Statistically, just having a parent in prison gives these children more than a 50 percent chance that they will spend some time locked up. The military is one of the few places for "at risk" kids to find discipline and structure.

Behind me sits a fourteen-year-old African American named Taj. Yes, as in Mahal. The writer in me can't help but think, How am I going to come up with better names than these when I write something about this day? There's even a kid on board with a name straight out of literature that is as instantaneously recognizable as, say, Aragorn, from *The Lord of the Rings*. And so I'll call him Aragorn, keeping the spirit of his name and protecting his privacy at the same time. I decide to use that as my guide when I rename the kids in print. Their mothers may be incarcerated, but they loved them enough to carefully and creatively name their children.

Jacqueline introduces a journalist and a photographer from the *Contra Costa Times* on board who are working on a story about Get on the Bus for Sunday's paper. Jacqueline tells everyone that if they want to speak with the press, they can, and that their identities will be protected unless they give permission otherwise. She introduces me as a "nice lady who is writing a book on prisoner's families."

"Oh, I want to talk to her," I hear a woman say a couple of seats behind me. Volunteers hand out goody bags with games and coloring books depending on the age and sex of the child. I note that the bags have the names of the children's mothers on them. After the introductions are over, I get up, lean over my seat, and try to engage Taj in conversation, but he's shy. He's carefully dressed in sharp green-and-white basketball clothes with matching sneakers; even his hair is neatly trimmed. His posture is straight, more suitable for church than a field trip. But then this is no ordinary bus ride. He's traveling alone.

I sit down again and watch the California hills roll along as we make our way through the Central Valley. Here and there patches of windmill farms, a source of alternative energy, dot the landscape. I have only been on this stretch of highway once before; it was on the last leg of my cross-country drive when I moved out here from New York almost four years ago. I think a lot about where I have come in those years. I think a lot about how Rory, Mr. Number 9, has helped me to grow and how I wouldn't be here without him.

Eventually, I get up again and start walking to the back of the bus. The woman who said she wanted to talk with me is sitting behind Taj, and I step out of the aisle and in front of the empty seat next to him, so that I can speak with her. "Is this okay?" I ask Taj first. "Sure," he says with a shrug.

The black woman behind him introduces herself as Lisa. She says she is forty-seven, my big sister's age, I think, but she looks much older than Cindy. She's been in and out of the very prison where her daughter is held. The warden just recently approved Lisa's request to visit. "Now they've got eight women in a room," she tells me. "It didn't used to be." She doesn't give any detail about her own criminal past, but she says she turned her life around because "I got tired of being away watching my daughter grow up in pictures and calling up on Christmas and birthdays. My sister passed away on me the last time."

Taj is playing with a wooden puzzle, but I sense he is paying attention to our conversation. When Lisa's sister died of kidney disease, she was approved and then unapproved to attend the funeral. "I only had six days to the gate," she says. Taj offers up his mom's release, September 9, 2008, like it was his own graduation date.

Lisa continues to introduce her grandkids: a seven-year-old angel with braids adorned with white clips and twisties; a nine-year-old boy, who says he is going to write a book of his own; and twelve-year-old Ty, who worms his way into my heart immediately when he flashes me a lady-killer smile. He tells me they are going to have a pool party for his brother's birthday this summer and that they once went to Disneyland for his birthday. Right now the children live with Lisa, but Ty says they have stayed with lots of relatives over the years.

I tell them that I am going to try to meet some other people on the bus and promise to come back later.

In the front of the bus I approach Skyler's grandfather, a white man who looks Scandinavian. As it turns out, Robert is Polish—and Catholic, which he makes a point of letting me know. He drove up from San Jose early that morning. He owns an auto repair shop there. His daughter, Pearl, has only been in prison a few months and is serving three years for a drug-related charge. I realize that no one is going to get too specific about what crime led to the incarceration of their daughters and mothers. Even when I push a little, they are vague. And I decide to just let them tell me what they want to, because those doing time on the outside navigate a minefield of judgment every day. And this is their special Mother's Day.

"She was in a gang," Robert says. "I have eight kids, and their mother went south, too. So I raised them on my own." He pauses to look at Skyler sitting in the window seat next to him. She plays with two Barbie dolls and is immersed in the conversation she creates for them and oblivious to ours. "She's been living with me since she was eleven months old."

"Hey, Skyler," I say, "how old are you?" She looks up at me with her wide-spaced eyes through blond curls that have fallen out of a pink barrette and juts out her right hand holding up three fingers.

Although a little quiet for a group of kids, the atmosphere on the bus is upbeat. The volunteers thought of everything, right down to the plastic bags needed to bring anything into the prison. The kids mingle and show off their artwork or toys. As we get off the freeway I notice that Ty's little sister is sitting next to Taj, laughing. He's counting her twisties, which number twenty.

Ty took my seat while I was up, so I sit next to him as we drive through an area off the freeway lined with citrus groves. He's been to see his mother before, so he's not nervous. (Not that he'd admit it to me even if he was, I think.) Instead, he impresses me with his smarts.

"You know those Christmas trees?" he asks.

"Evergreens?" I take a good look at him; he's got cropped hair like Taj, but he's still got a little baby fat that plumps out his cheeks.

"Nah," he says.

"Douglas fir?" I try again.

"Yeah, them," he says with a huge smile that I think could actually light up a Christmas tree. "They have enough vitamin C in just one little piece that if you eat it, you will have all the energy you need for the rest of the day." He smiles a mile wide, so pleased with himself that I can't help but adore this kid.

He tells me he learned about that at science camp. The citrus groves part and we drive into a concrete prison compound entrance. I've checked out the two women's prisons that are part of this bus trip on the California Department of Corrections Web site. As we drive past a stone wall with "Central California Women's Facility" on it, I remember that the driving directions on the Web site actually said, "Right onto Road 24. First prison on your right." In 1990 the state cut out over six hundred acres of citrus groves to make room for the largest women's prison in the United States. Designed for approximately two thousand inmates, it houses over three thousand, including fourteen on California's only female death row. No women have been executed in California since the state reinstated the death penalty in 1977.

None of the children today are visiting anyone on death row.

I ask Ty if his mother is here.

"Nah, she's in the other one." He means the other prison for women down the road called Valley State. He says it's been about a year since he was here last.

A few families get off with some volunteers at this prison, and then we continue farther down the citrus-grove-lined road to a very similar-looking prison compound that is Valley State

Prison for Women. Built in 1995, VSPW was designed for approximately two thousand inmates and houses almost thirty-seven hundred. "It has grown to be one of the largest women's prisons in the world," according to its Web site.

Our Oakland bus is only one of twenty-four in the special Friday Mother's Day convoy. The buses come from all corners of the state; many of these children left before daybreak to make it here to the Central Valley. It takes nearly an hour to get us all processed through.

The Get on the Bus organizers have prepped the families well for their entrance into prison, so there are very few hiccups as we go through the metal detectors. I hang back with a volunteer named Harold whom I met back in the fall when I attended that same conference where I met Sister Suzanne. He's in his early thirties and works for an organization that helps inmates and their families both plan for and cope with a prisoner's release. Harold's an ex-con; he did six years in San Quentin for attempted murder. After he did his time, he put himself through college one class at a time. He clearly loves his work.

From the prison's perspective Harold's an NIP, Notoriously Important Person, because he did time. Now six years out, and long done with parole, he no longer is required to carry his prison release card, but he carries it anyway. "It's just easier," he says.

As the series of gates mechanically open and close to let us past the death fences and razor wire, I notice something strikingly different about this prison: there's a patch of plush green grass *inside*, along the path to the visiting center building.

The inside of the visiting center resembles a barn, with high, sloped ceilings. But this barn is made of concrete and painted institutional gray-blue. We walk toward a huge room off to the right that is at least six times the size of the visiting room at Pelican Bay. A mural of "women of the world" decorates the far wall. Since all of this was arranged in advance, the inmates who signed up for Get on the Bus are already inside the visiting area. Some clog the entrance into the room as they clamor to get a first glimpse of their kids. Others have already reunited. It feels like a school cafeteria in mid-mealtime and sounds like a playground. Outside on the patio—grass again—the prison staff are cooking hot dogs on a couple of gas grills.

The room swallows me up, and I lose sight of the people from the bus. Never mind, I think, there are lots of reunions to watch. "Is that the San Diego bus?" someone asks. "She look just like her mother," I hear one inmate say to another. A group of four women, all dressed in their prison-issue jeans and blue-and-white baseball-style T-shirts, coo at an infant girl with one of those elastic bows on her hairless head. The room is awash with blue and yellow: the moms in blue and their families in bright yellow T-shirts provided by Catholic Charities.

I'm wearing black pants and a tailored pink shirt.

The vibe in the room is just too positive for me to even wonder what the mothers did to be sent to prison. But then I spot one slender white inmate with a thin blond French braid with what looks like a permanent scowl on her face. And I think how I wouldn't want to run into her in a dark alley.

I wander around the room, which holds at least one hundred inmates already with their children or waiting for them, but my eyes keep coming back to the scowling woman. She is concentrating on the door. Suddenly she leans forward on her knees, looks down, then quickly gets up with tears in her eyes and brings her hands to cover her mouth as she catches sight of a blond girl of about five dressed in a frilly violet dress, complete with white tights and white patent leather shoes.

The little girl swooshes her head back and forth searching around the room for her mother. The woman with the French braid rocks back and forth with her hands up at her mouth as in prayer and waits for her daughter to see her. Then the little girl's eyes pop out wide and her mouth drops open as if the sight of her mother is like Christmas, her birthday, and Easter all rolled into one. Her mother kneels down and the girl leaps into her arms, nearly knocking her over. The mother picks her daughter up and extends the hug to her own mother. The girl is giggling but the women have tears in their eyes.

Paul Simon's "Mother and Child Reunion" plays in my head as I watch reunion after reunion.

I spot Taj sitting at a table engaged in an animated conversation with his mom. She leans forward and he sits on the edge of one chair with his leg sprawled across the other one, facing her. I come upon Lisa's family, already engaged in craft projects, an extra provided for this special visiting day. She introduces me to her daughter, Nina.

"Oh, they told me about you," says Nina, extending her hand, which was wrapped around her daughter with the twenty twisties in her hair who is sitting between her mother's legs on the same chair.

I tell her how much I enjoyed meeting her children and how nice it is to meet her, too. "This one here's real smart," I say, putting my hand on Ty's shoulder. "He was teaching me a thing or two about science on the bus. You've got great kids." Usually when I say that to any kid's mother I feel a pang of jealousy, but all I feel here and now is compassion. I feel honored that her kids were so open with me, and I loved how her family seemed to adopt Taj as the miles rolled away on our early-morning prison journey.

I think I might cry, but this time not for myself, and so I take my leave and walk around the room.

Skyler's grandfather invites me to sit with them. His daughter Pearl is twenty-six; she has long blond hair worn straight to the middle of her back. She's average in size, with a bit of a belly. She has a couple of pimples on her face.

At first I think Pearl doesn't want me to sit with them, because she did not even acknowledge me when her father introduced us.

"It's been rough on her," says Robert.

"This is good for me," says Pearl, looking around the room and barely holding back tears. Skyler clings to her, and she holds her daughter tightly, but her focus is on the entire room and she's lost in thought. The joy and the love that are so palpable on this day affect her strongly. She apologizes for not paying attention to me. Robert tells Pearl that her brother is going to come and visit. "Nate's coming?" she says, snapping out of her thoughts. Then she invites me to join them for lunch.

On the way to the lunch line I stop to visit with the family from the back of our bus. Melissa, a white woman with light brown hair pulled back into a ponytail, brought her three granddaughters—ranging in age from eighteen to twelve—to visit their mom. The twelve-year-old has Down syndrome. She hugs me and won't let go, as I meet her mother, Grace. Grace's oldest daughter has two boys of her own: a toddler and an infant (the source of the crying on the bus). The mother/grandmother inmate has already signed love notes on all of their yellow

T-shirts. The girls and the infant are all blond. The toddler, a
brunette cherub with shocking blue eyes, tries to squirm out of
his grandma's arms as she shakes my hand.

When I met them earlier on the bus, Melissa explained that
all of the children live in various parts of the state with family
members. This day is their reunion. The way they sit huddled
together occupying just a corner of the table, it is as if they want
to absorb every touch and every sound they can with their lim-
ited amount of time. I do not want to intrude, so I say hello and
then a quick good-bye.

On my way to join Skyler and her family on the lunch line, I
overhear Emanuel's mother ask him about school. He starts saying his numbers in Spanish. I notice that tears teeter just below
the surface of many of these smiles. Pearl's dad massages her back
as they stand in line. Skyler hangs on to her mother's right leg.

The food's pretty simple. Foot-longs, chips, and soda. When
Skyler drops hers, I go get her another hot dog and the people
handling the food don't mind at all. We say grace before we eat
and it's the same prayer I still say before meals with my parents:
"Bless us, oh Lord, for these thy gifts, which we are about to receive . . . " And then Pearl just talks—it's not so much a conversation as a scattered laundry list with very little detail. She says
she was pregnant when she got arrested, which her father says he
didn't know. He doesn't look too surprised at the news.

"I guess my pregnancies are every three years," she says casu-
ally, as if discussing out-of-wedlock babies with her Catholic father is no big deal. A quiet man, he seems willing to simply
listen; he probably found out years ago that judging her was fu-
tile. She says she didn't even see a doctor until after she was sentenced and sent here. By then, she was four months along and

the baby had "lodged itself" in one of her fallopian tubes. She says she had an operation and the baby died.

I know that the baby could not have moved into her fallopian tube, and that what she is talking about is a life-threatening condition for the mother. But I am not sure if Pearl comprehends what really happened or if she just doesn't have the vocabulary to properly explain it.

She continues with the laundry list. "So I only have one tube now," she says.

"She's had it rough," her father says again. I think it's his standard line.

I let a few minutes go by, and then I say I'll give them some privacy.

I stop by and introduce myself to Taj's mom. I can see where he gets his looks from. She is tall like Taj, with clear dark skin. I wonder how she straightens her hair in prison. I can't quite peg her age. I'd guess late twenties or early thirties. So many of the women inmates, I've found, look older than they are. I tell her that I think Taj is a terrific kid and then move along, not wanting to take up too much of their precious time alone.

Again, I feel no jealous pangs. If anything, I am embarrassed to have become so self-pitying.

Much of the afternoon I spend talking with Harold, watching and comparing what we've seen on this very special Friday Mother's Day. Of the more than three hundred visitors that day, I saw only one family that included a father sitting at the table. "Look," I say to Harold, pointing outside to where a mother is chasing her boys around on the grass and two little girls try to do cartwheels. "I wonder if those girls came together, or found each other like kids do," I say.

When I run into Ty at the vending machines he asks me for

50 cents. I had already given away the few dollars I had brought with me and it kills me to say, "I'm sorry, sweetie." Somehow it feels right to call kids I barely know "sweetie" all day. Unde-terred, Ty asks one of the guards for the change, and he digs into his pocket and gives it to him.

For one bright shining day, these kids who normally carry around the stigma associated with having a mother in prison get to feel special. And they see their mothers feeling special, like mothers again.

The girl in the frilly violet dress stands on a chair, hanging on to her mother's back. There's a sizable hole in her tights on her left knee. And her hair is falling out of her pig-tails. Her mother, Roxanne, tells me she is a lifer. Maybe that explains the scowl I saw on her face earlier. Her daughter's name is Jewel. "I lost a tooth," she proclaims, jutting out her chin to show me the gap in her bottom front teeth.

"I pulled it out," her mother says.

I say something about how I remember my father snatching a loose tooth out when I was a kid. It's a universal experience: a kid's fear giving way in the instant a trusted parent snatches a tooth like that. I tell Roxanne how happy I am that she got to take her daughter's tooth out. That she got to be there, for that moment.

Roxanne takes the tooth out of her jeans pocket and shows it to me. She says she wants family visits so that she can spend time alone with her daughter doing normal things. But lifers don't get family visits. She is not even sure the guards will let her keep her daughter's tooth when the women are strip-searched after the visit and are sent back to their cells.

Jewel tells me that the Tooth Fairy is going to come tonight and leave her money even though her mommy has the tooth, because she's special and the Tooth Fairy knows it.

Visiting ends at 3:00 p.m., and about a half hour before, the mood in the room changes drastically. It had been so pleasant. Not even "bathroom break" announcements interrupted the visits, because the prison relaxed its rules for the day and let the women come and go at will, accompanied by a guard. And so when the guard announces ten more minutes, it sends a shock, and a plague of tears descends on almost everyone there.

Finally the guard says time's up and instructs all inmates to go out on the patio, *now*. It sounds cruel, but how else can they end this day, except quickly, like tearing off a Band-Aid? The women tear themselves away from their families and go outside. They line up against the glass wall, while their children press up against it on the other side. A two-year-old Latino boy stands on a table next to the glass and smudges it with his tiny hands. He kisses his mother's lips through the glass barrier. "I love you, Mommy," he says, as he giggles and dances for her. His four-year-old sister sits on her grandmother's lap in a chair near the boy. The girl cries inconsolably. And the grandmother gently pats the girl's back, as women have handled hysterical children for ages.

I walk out of the prison with Skyler and her grandfather. Skyler skips and her grandfather says she is too young to understand much.

Our bus is the first to leave because, sadly, Esmeralda's mother had committed some kind of infraction that morning, and so their visit was canceled. Instead of hot dogs and hugs, the twelve-year-old girl sat on the bus with her grandmother all day. Esmeralda is quiet as we board the bus, and stays that way for much of the trip home. The other children's reactions vary. Many of them are used to bouncing back, I think, and the younger ones, like Skyler, have no idea what is really going on.

Each child gets a teddy bear and a special letter from Mom for the ride home. Reese cuddles up with his furry white bear in the seat across the aisle. Taj and Ty scoff at the stuffed animals and play Battleship in the seat behind me. Emanuel cries quietly in his aunt's arms. His mother wrote on his T-shirt, "This little boy made with love by . . . ," and she signed it.

When I walk to the back of the bus the girl with Down syndrome stops me for a hug. Once I can break away, I go all the way to the back, where Jacqueline is overseeing the teddy bear giveaways. She hands me a soft brown bear. I try to decline the gift, but Jacqueline insists. When I walk back toward my seat the Down syndrome girl stops me for another hug. Like Skyler, she is unaware and playful, even.

I have always found the resilience of children striking, but I am in awe of these kids. Even Esmeralda perks up and is laughing, largely because Taj is egging Ty on to go and talk to her. She smiles with the brilliance of any twelve-year-old girl who knows a cute twelve-year-old boy is watching her. It's hilarious. Ty keeps saying to Taj that he'll make his move, but then doesn't. Finally, I poke my face between the seats and ask him point-blank: "So are you going to talk to her or not?" I surprise him, but he knows I mean it kindly. He laughs and smiles that lady-killer smile that landed so deeply in my heart, and I hope I remember this full feeling of love for a kid I barely know. And I hope that I never feel sorry for myself again for not having kids.

"You're blushing," I tease Ty.

"No, I'm not," he insists, but he knows I've got him pegged.

"Hey, can I ask you guys something, but don't laugh at me," I say. Of course they guffaw when I ask who they are listening to on Taj's boom box.

"I don't even know myself," Ty says, unable to stop laughing.

"So then why are you laughing at *me*?" I say.

When Taj tells us the group's name I pretend to recognize it, but I am not fooling them one bit.

It's after 7:00 p.m. when we arrive back at St. Leander's. There are a lot of hugs and "God bless you's" as we say our good-byes. And then we go back to our lives.

On my drive home I think, Oh, Sister Suzanne, what have you done to me? Okay, I see all of this need. And I just don't know what to do.

I stop at the convenience store to buy half-and-half for my morning coffee. I hope the Indian store owner, who has the same birthday as me, is there so I can tell someone about this amazing day. But when I walk in the store I see his sister behind the counter and her daughter dressed in pink sitting on it. I think she is probably three and a half, Skyler's age. I say she looks very tired. And when she says nothing back, her mother touches her daughter's face to see if she is hot, like mothers have done with their children forever. "You're not feeling up to snuff," I say, using the phrase my mother always used when she would look in my eyes and know I was coming down with something before I showed even a single symptom. I think, How do mothers just know?

As I go to leave I hear a faint "bye" from the girl. I walk away

thinking how this little girl will go home tonight and be com-
forted and cared for by her mom, and how the other kids I met
today will fall asleep missing their moms.

Then I go home to my empty apartment. I lie in bed with the
faces of the children and their mothers in prison blues whirling
in my head. When the tears come, I know I cry for anyone who
feels an emptiness in life, and I feel less alone.

I am not sure how or in what capacity I will get involved, but I
now know I will work with children whose mothers are in
prison. And I can't wait to tell Rory about it.

I didn't have to wait long, because on Sunday morning he
calls me instead of his own mother on Mother's Day.

The tears rush out of me without warning. Within Rory's
voice, his heart, his mind—resides the place where all of my
feelings can swirl around freely—and I cry cradled in the
knowledge that he understands everything churning inside
of me without my saying anything. That just makes me cry
even more.

"Rory, how can I ever thank you for loving me so well?" I say,
once I can speak. I gush about the bus trip, and all the kids and
their moms. I tell him that I know I am going to do something
with kids like that, and it feels good. "But I've got to get rid of
the bitterness I still feel so sharply," I say, crying again. "Because
it can never be like this is second best for these kids—like they
are to fill *my* void. They deserve so much more."

That night I sleep with my two bears: Frankie, who holds the
dreams of my past, and this new brown bear from the bus, who
holds unimagined dreams of my future. I want to name him

after every child on the bus, but I name him Aragorn, in honor of all their unique names. And I go to sleep thinking that if my new dream bear wants to bring movie Aragorn in the form of Viggo Mortensen to my bed, that would be okay with me.

The next day there is a card from Rory sitting in my mailbox. Within the heart made of a flower garland on the cover, it says "No Special Occasion." I recognize the penciled printing inside as coming from the man who knows me like no one else.

My Beautiful Angel . . .

There is something that I have been meaning to say to you for the longest time, yet I was unsure if you were to a point in your healing where you could receive it with the love and sincerity I intend . . .

But now, my love, you are becoming whole right before me; you are growing in strength and beauty, more and more, each time I am able to gaze upon you . . .

And so, Bridget Mary Kinsella, this upcoming Sunday I want you to know a truth I mean with every part of me, with every fiber of my being, with my heart and soul, with so much <u>love</u> [underlined twice] that the very word could never hold it or truly describe it . . .

Which is this: It is a precious and amazing gift to <u>create</u> [underlined twice] new life, but it is every bit as amazing and far more rare to be able to <u>complete</u> [underlined twice] a life that already exists . . . Yet, my love, this is just what you have done . . . And for this, there can never be a soul who loves you more than I . . . I shall forever cherish you.

In Truth and Love,

Rory Francis Mehan

P.S. So we're both angels, huh? I <u>love</u> [underlined twice]
that. It makes me think of our spirits making love high up
in the sky changing colors as we fall, like eagles do.

I cuddle my brown bear of new dreams and reread the card. And I have to admit that this prison journey, which started out as the love of a man for a woman and could end with the well-being of a child, might just lead to happily ever after, after all.

CHAPTER 12

THIRTY-NINE DAYS

When the inevitable happened, only once did Rory show any sign of anger about my leaving our fantasy life behind. His shoes gave him away.

"What's with the sneakers?" I ask in the middle of a visit about a month after the next New Year, when Rory wished for me to dance.

He looks down at his pristine white sneakers and then back up at me, embarrassed. The inmates are not really supposed to wear sneakers in the visiting room, but most do. I prefer when Rory wears the brown boots that are regulation-issue, not because they conform to the rules, but because they add a refined quality to his prison blues.

"Well," he starts to explain.

I know that the months since I went to prison with the kids of incarcerated women have been hard on Rory. I've spent most of my time getting my life in order, especially my financial situation. Under new management at my magazine, my job became full-time. If I was going to open my heart to a child in need, I needed to build a steadier foundation. Giving up the dream of having a child of my own was the hardest thing I have ever done. Now that I have seen so much need, I accept and embrace my future role as foster parent or mentor to a child whose mother is in prison. Still, I wasn't quite sure where I wanted to put down roots. Sometimes I wondered if I should go back east to be with my family.

Meanwhile, Rory worked on his novels, multitasking worlds and missing me. Between my work and his lockdowns, my visits had become sporadic, stretching out to every three or four months.

Rory was patient, but he wasn't a saint. And the shoes I preferred to sneakers bore the brunt of his pain.

"Well," he starts to explain again. The prison had been slammed down, on and off, for months. When he got locked down yet again, Rory snapped, took the laces out of his boots, and threw one boot out onto the tier. "Then everyone started chuckin' stuff out there, and I chucked out the other one," he says. When his young celly reminded him that I liked those boots, Rory snapped back, "Yeah, well, she doesn't visit much anymore."

Then after all the other inmates cluttered the tier with toilet paper, rotten food, tattered clothing, anything they could get their hands on, Rory started to regret throwing away the shoes. "I looked out and saw them sitting there like two pathetic dogs, lying in the middle of all this crap with their tongues hangin' out," he says, sticking out his tongue and gesturing with his hands at either side of his mouth.

The image and the way he describes the scene crack me up. My laughter fills the visiting room. "You should get angry," I say. "It serves me right!" I am warmed in my laughter and the wonderful feeling of being content in his company, not wishing for more and not seeing it as anything less than the magical connection we've made it.

Up until this point, he has denied me nothing I've asked of him.

When he writes to me after the visit he doesn't talk about our discussing Don DeLillo's *The Body Artist* or his discovering the wonders of key lime pie out of the vending machine. No, he writes about the shoes:

> *Now I am laughing at my own trepidation all this last month, because I knew when you asked on our next visit then I'd have to tell you about The Great Shoe Rebellion of '06! Yet when I did tell you, you laughed and laughed, such an amazing delicious sound, and now I am laughing remembering it.*
>
> *The beauty of your laughter. Its sound of your new spirit. Its color in your skin. The happy tears of joy amplifying your eyes so that I can just fall right into you for the rest of our lives and never hit bottom. Just fall and fall forever . . .*
>
> *. . . I am so glad you are okay, pretty one.*
>
> *Worrying bleeds so much energy.*
>
> *I will wrap this up for now to send it out into the great big crowded world of broken and wounded souls to find the one I know most intimately of all. A soul that carries inside of it the "light and scent and beauty of a thousand hidden flowers."*
>
> *Do you remember the poem I wrote that in?*
>
> *They are all blooming now, my love.*
>
> *All of those hidden flowers blooming.*
>
> *I knew they were there all along.*

———

That summer I took a week off to go up to Crescent City, figuring I'd spend two weekends in a row with Rory to make up for months of being away. He had told me a couple of times on the phone and in his letters that he had something he needed to discuss with me in person without the eyes and ears of the prison between us.

I told him that I'd try to guess what it was.

"There's no way you can guess *this*," he said, with a strange, almost hollow laugh one night on the phone.

So a mystery hangs over me as I take the familiar twists and turns up Interstate 101 once again. The routine remains the same, but I no longer need its comfort. Half-listening to National Public Radio on the way up, I hear Robert Siegel read a letter sent in by a nine-year-old boy. "When someone loves you, they say your name differently," he wrote.

Wow, I think to myself, how perceptive is that? When you think about it, it applies for all kinds of love—filial, friendly, or romantic. Even years after my grandmother's death, I can still hear the echo of her Italian voice calling me "Bridgitta" like no one else ever will. My father's tenor is like none other when he sings, "Bridget Mary, me darlin'." From the very beginning in our correspondence, long before we even met, Rory managed to say my name on paper in a way that conveyed an extraordinary love. As we continued on our journey together and in our separate lives, his love only grew stronger—even when I had to force myself to back away from it.

Before I left for this week I realized that, three years into our relationship, we've only actually spent thirty-nine days in each other's company.

"Thirty-nine days?" Rory says, when I relate this to him on our visit. "Huh." He holds my hands in his on the table but looks off in the distance lost in his own thoughts. I ask him what he needs to talk with me about. He reminds me that I was going to guess. So I tell him the only thing I could come up with: that he wanted to ask me if he could name me as the person to contact if anything happened to him.

It's not a pleasant thought, I say, but the truth is, he could get knifed or worse at any moment. I thought he might prefer if I were the one who would break the news to his mother, whom I've met but do not really know.

"Oh, that's nothin'," he says. When I press him to tell me what is on his mind, he suggests that we go outside. So we sit at the cement picnic table where we opened our hearts to each other three years ago. He holds my left hand in his and picks at the jagged top layer of cement that we've picked at before.

"I guess the best way to say it is to just say it," he says, looking up at me and taking my right hand in his. He stretches his back and then pulls in his shoulders and leans toward me. "I felt something in the back of my throat, and I knew what it was. I went to the doctor, and, yeah, it's cancer."

The big things in life never feel like they are happening.

"I'm not going to get it treated," he says, relaxing his posture and stroking my hands now grasping his left hand.

I have no words, but Rory does.

"I had this great opening line, but you needed to know to understand what it meant."

He's talking about opening lines? He's thirty-three, dying of cancer, and he's talking about opening lines!

"I've decided to keep my cancer—that's the line," he says, looking into my eyes as if to tell me it's all going to be okay. "But I couldn't tell you like that."

Finally my tears come. I still cannot speak. He asks if I understand why he doesn't want treatment. I nod my head and cry more. If I were serving life without parole, I'd make the same choice.

"I think I came up with a great ending for your book," he says, wiping away my tears and caressing my cheek. "I think I just gave you *Tuesdays with Morrie*."

I snort through salty tears now laced with laughter. "Oh my God," I say, recovering my voice. "You really *will* do anything for me."

I laugh and I cry simultaneously, as he assures me that the doctor said that it is still very early. Suddenly the idea of time makes me gasp and cry harder. I try to explain through gulps for air that I am not crying to mourn for the time we will not have, but in awe of the very little bit of it we've shared and what we've done with it.

"I just got your hands to stop shaking," he says. I feel a shiver in my body, but can't help but laugh.

Once I calm down Rory explains that he felt something in his throat for a while. He found out about it two months ago. He says the doctor wasn't very nice to him at first. "I guess she was having a bad day, treating another inmate in shackles," he says. She insisted he had strep throat or some infection. Rory mimes her actions as he tells me she groused before she shined a little light into his mouth and then her jaw dropped.

Rory leans forward and points to what looks like a white slash in his right tonsil. He closes his mouth and contracts his throat, as he has probably been doing for months, feeling the cancerous mass from the inside.

Another prison doctor confirmed the diagnosis and made him sign some form about declining treatment. "They charged me five dollars for the appointment because it wasn't medically necessary," he tells me, because he refused treatment. He and the doctor got a good chuckle at the irony.

"Are you okay?" I ask, now mostly composed.

"I'm fine. I feel great, actually."

Rory grieved for his life the first time he lost it, when he took it away himself by committing murder.

"I can't wait to see what's next," he says. "And I hope it's like nothin' that anyone ever thought of." He smiles his crooked grin. He tells me he worried that I might get mad at him for refusing treatment, but that he thought I'd come back tomorrow and understand.

I understand already.

When the time comes to say good-bye for the day we kiss outside by our cement table with a passion that has been missing since I backed away from our fantasies. It's a kiss that says, "I know who you are like no one else."

When I walk out of the prison with the other women it's hard to act as if nothing is wrong. But Rory doesn't want to tell anyone until his mother can come and visit. So I talk with Naomi and Laurie about how Rory's celly is getting transferred and that he is looking for a new one. Only then do I notice that Pamela was not there, and I am grateful for her absence. She'd want to grab dinner with me later and I am not sure I could hold myself together, let alone eat.

I wish Naomi and Laurie safe driving back to the reservation and take the long way along the beach back to the motel. When I go into the office to get extra cream and sugar for my morning coffee, as I always do, Sonia, one of the owners of the Travelodge, comes out from the back office, as she always does. After three years of staying in her motel, we have become friends, and I think it is okay if I tell her about Rory.

Sonia's husband, Paul, comes out from the back room when he hears me crying. They are Chinese immigrants, and Sonia says that in Buddhism death is not the end. Even so, it is a shock and they both offer sympathy.

I read for a while in my room, but I am restless. It's too early for dinner, and I know the Catholic church has a 5:00 p.m. Mass, so I decide to attend. Mass always reminds me of my mother. I arrive late and slip into a pew halfway up the right side aisle. I hadn't been to Mass in a couple of months, so I am not sure what part of the Gospel story will be in this evening's readings. When the priest reads of the Transfiguration of Christ, I think the timing is perfect. I look over my right shoulder and notice I am sitting next to the fifth Station of the Cross, where Simon of Cyrene helps Jesus carry the cross on the way to His crucifixion.

"We have been each other's Simon of Cyrene," I silently pray to Rory. I am not sure what I feel, but it overwhelms me, and I fight back tears. As I sing the last hymn, "How Great Thou Art," I think of attending Mass with my parents back in their retirement community in New Jersey. Whenever there is time to fill at the end of communion their organist plays "How Great Thou Art," and even though the lyrics aren't printed in their hymnals, so ingrained are the words that the elderly congregation sings the hymn with confidence and verve. Somehow I usually wind up between my parents after communion, and standing there alone in St. Joseph's singing, I embrace my mother and father's comfort from three thousand miles away.

The next day I recount this for Rory and lament how he will never meet my parents, especially my mother.

"I know her echo," he says.

I am wearing a tea-length, dark blue silk, feminine, church-going dress with a small, pale yellow pattern of forget-me-nots in the fabric. Buttons go from the nape of my neck to below my knee. Although it has long been one of my favorites, I seldom wear it, because it reminds me of Alexei's mother coming to visit us in Michigan when we were in the middle of so much turmoil. It was Mother's Day weekend, and I remember going to sleep that Saturday night crying because I wondered if I'd ever have a Mother's Day of my own. The next morning when Alexei took his mother out for breakfast, I wore the dress to Mass to cheer myself up. But when the priest asked all the mothers to stand up and be recognized, and I looked at the children all dressed up in their best clothes, I got out of there as quickly as I could. Alexei might remember our time together fondly; he has that luxury. But like every memory of my marriage, this dress was tainted.

Several times Rory puffs up his chest when he looks at me in the dress as we stand near the microwave or take a stroll in our stone garden. "You know I've got some business with those buttons," he says. I don't bother to explain the history of the dress because the love in his eyes reclaims it for me without my asking. Somehow I feel whole and I know he does, too.

Cancer is really an angel of mercy for us both, he tells me. He admits that he wasn't sure how he'd handle my letting go completely, as was his plan all along.

He sits with a huge grin on his face as he talks about his

theory of consciousness. "I think this is all gonna seem like kindergarten when it's over," he says. He thinks that our "spirits," for lack of a better word, are like students picking college courses who choose lives on earth with lessons we wish to learn. Then the other spirits we are connected with watch us from above on a sort of closed-circuit television system. They root for us and take odds, like in a heavenly version of offtrack betting.

"They'd say, 'Man, you really messed up that semester,'" he jokes about his criminal life. And as they watched him fall and do his time, they'd gradually notice that monitors 22 and 31 are starting to play the same thing. They can't believe their eyes, he continues. "And anyone who had their money on us, that's a long shot that really paid off!"

On the second day knowing that Rory will die, the only thing that makes me cry is the thought of how well we have loved each other and how so much stood in the way of our even meeting.

Sitting at our cement table outside, I ask Rory how much time he wants left. He was going to ask for ten years, but that seemed too long. "I didn't say that out loud," he says, looking skyward. He wants enough time to finish a couple of his novels in progress and a new one, too. He started writing a story in which his character killed his abusive father and spends ten years in prison. After his release he goes to care for his mother, who has Alzheimer's. Listening to her, he cannot know what is real and what is affected by her disease, but he realizes that he took something from her by killing his father.

I think he wants to relive and reclaim his first memory of being a helpless child unable to stop his father from beating his mother. Through fiction he might finally melt the chunk of ice holding the single blade of grass that is his shame.

So, of our thirty-nine days, I ask, what was most important for him?

"How you made me want to be a man, when I've always hated men," he says without hesitation.

We are sitting next to the television area and the second *Lord of the Rings* movie is playing on the monitor. It's his favorite of the Peter Jackson trilogy. I share my theory of how it's everyone's favorite because at the end of the movie the story isn't over. He glances at the TV, watching for his favorite scene, when the guard announces a bathroom break.

I watch him on line against the wall talking with one of the other inmates, whom Rory has told me is a southern Mexican gang member. When Rory comes back to our table, he says to the southern Mexican, "It's comin' up!" Apparently, they are both waiting for the same scene.

He holds my hand and looks at the TV with his mouth hanging open. The Battle for Helm's Deep is nearly over on the screen, and all hope seems lost for the good guys.

"What are you thinking about?" I ask. But Rory's eyes remain transfixed to the movie. I turn my head to catch the moment when Aragorn, faced with their doom in battle, says to the king, "Ride out with me!" Basically, stand tall and go down fighting.

It's what Rory and his southern Mexican friend are waiting for. I look around the room and notice several other inmates are staring at the screen, taking in the cinematic moment of bravery and honor.

"C'mon, what are you thinking?" I ask again.

Rory snaps out of his trance and looks at me. "I've been trying to die right my whole life," he says, with his crooked smile on his face. "And now I may get my chance to do it."

He tells me he's already named his cancer "Jules," because of a quote from Shakespeare's *Julius Caesar*. He gives me his best shot at paraphrasing this: "Most men are cowards who die many times before their actual death; while the valiant among us never taste of death but once. . . . Of all the wonders I have heard it seems to me the most strange that men should know fear; seeing how death is a quite necessary end that shall come whenever it shall come."

Later, outside at our table, he asks me if I'm ready. Our songbird serenades us from its perch on the razor wire.

"Yes," I whisper. "As Gandhi said, 'Where there is love, there's life.' It's about time I did more than just visit with it." We both have tears in our eyes, because I am ready to live again, thanks to Rory's love. And when he dies we both know that I will carry our love on in my heart and bring its grace into whatever I do.

After I returned home, I woke up one Saturday morning and retrieved my wedding ring from its place in the bottom of my sock drawer.

I walked into a crowded jewelry store and felt no sadness as I watched couples shop for diamond love tokens. "I came to reclaim my wedding band," I said to the woman who stepped up to help me. She said yes, I could have something engraved that I didn't buy there, which made me think of *Breakfast at Tiffany's* again and Holly Golightly having a Cracker Jack ring engraved.

I played with my wedding ring on my right hand and told her the story of Rory and Bridget. "We will never be joined anywhere, except here," I said, holding up the white gold band with a yellow gold strand of forget-me-nots around it. "I am not going to marry him," I continued, putting the ring on my left hand. "You know, it always was a little tight. Can you stretch it?" I asked the saleswoman her name. "Well, Jill, how's that for irony, my marriage never really quite fit." We both laughed.

A few days later I felt a sense of joy as I examined the words only Rory and I (and Jill) know to be engraved in script inside this powerful band of gold. Jill was too polite to ask me what I planned to do with it, so I told her:

For now, I will wear it on my right hand, and when Rory dies, I will have this symbol to put aside. I might bury it at his grave, or toss it off of the Golden Gate Bridge. Or I might save it and give it to one of the children whose moms are in prison, that is, if I am lucky enough to affect one of their lives. With the words etched inside the ring, nothing will ever erase what it stands for: the union of two people who set each other free.

ACKNOWLEDGMENTS

I have always said that the greatest blessings in my life are the people I know. I feel like I should thank just about every person I've met when it comes to acknowledging who helped me with this book, but my publisher says the acknowledgments should not be longer than the manuscript.

I will begin by thanking my family, especially my parents. I know it hasn't always been easy for you to watch me move along on this challenging journey, but, Mom and Dad, you have helped me so much, and I have to say that I love our "adult" relationship. Whenever I come back to my life after spending time with you, I always tell people how much I just love my parents' company. If you weren't my parents, I'd want you to be.

Now my siblings, Lucinda, Joseph, Patrick, and Claire. We did a lot of loving and laughing together in the yellow brick house at 397 Main Street and beyond. Patrick may have gotten the most play on these pages (well, we know how Patrick can be), but that is only because my experiences with him fit in with the story I needed to tell here. The thing is, I love each of you deeply and individually. Being the youngest is a little like being the family pet (but in a good way); how you've all loved me, spoiled me rotten for life when it came to how I should be treated. And you have no idea how much I appreciate your support as I started writing this book. Even Cindy, whose response to hearing I had a relationship with a man in prison was, "Oh, Bridget!"

While writing this book it became very clear to me that I come from an extraordinary family. Nieces, nephews, uncles, cousins—we've got members by the dozens. I have dedicated this book to you all because I would not be who I am without you and your love. And a special nod must be made to my Italian grandmother, Lucia, from whom all of my storytelling abilities stem.

Speaking of families, I want to thank my second family, my *Publishers Weekly* family. I wish I could list the entire masthead here to thank you all for your support and friendship. I hope you all know how much I appreciate you. A special thank-you to Sara Nelson, editor-in-chief, for going "above and beyond" to support my writing this book. Also, thanks to Jim Milliot for his special patience. And to Michael Coffey and Robin Lenz, who have been in charge of massaging the words that make it into the magazine for the fourteen years I have written for it, you have taught me so much about writing. (Yes, Robin, even when we quibbled over copyedits, I was listening.) A special thanks to John Mutter, now the head of *Shelf Awareness*, for so much more than teaching me how to write a lead.

My other real writing education occurred when I attended Columbia University's Graduate School of Journalism. I have to thank the entire class of 1998, because getting through that program is really a group effort. But I offer my special thanks to the teachers and students in my Master's class with Carole Agus, Judith Crist's writing class, and the radio workshop with Joe Richman and Ann Cooper.

I made some of my best friends at Columbia, who have encouraged me more than I could explain. Thank you, Daniel Paul Simmons III, Diederik van Hoogstraten, Mareike Schomerus, Lila LaHood, Trevor Butterworth, Cecile Daurat, Ivor Hanson (I'd be your twin if you didn't already have one), and Georg Szalai.

My top thanks go to my agent and friend Amy Rennert. I still remember when I told you about this book idea and how supportive you have been every step of the way. Oh, and you found me the perfect editor and publisher!

What can I say about my editor, Julia Pastore? You have been my champion all along and caught me on every single fudge and misdirection. I will forever keep next to my desk the encouraging note you sent while I was writing. And I offer my thanks to everyone at Harmony Books, from publisher Shaye Areheart, for her amazing support, to the designers, copyeditors, sales reps, and promotions people for all of their dedication and talent.

Some of my favorite people in publishing actually "passed" on this book. As strange as it sounds, I want to thank you who rejected the book, because so many of you (and you know who you are) still gave me your support and even your time as I worked through the publishing process. I shall never forget your gracious encouragement, but, sorry, that doesn't mean I will favor your books in print.

I send a special thank-you to the booksellers across the country who have encouraged me to write this book, especially Elaine and Bill Petrocelli at Book Passage in Corte Madera,

California, who were the first to read any of the manuscript. Booksellers, along with librarians, are our unsung national treasures.

When it comes to readers, however, I must thank my dynamic duo, Marissa Moss and Kathleen Caldwell, who read the book as I wrote it—and gave me immediate feedback. I never could have gotten the book done without your wonderful (and did I mention immediate?) insights and comments. You are so much more than good friends.

I am blessed with way too many friends to thank, but I hope you know how much I treasure you who know me well. I must give a special shout-out to the Fortieth Birthday "ladies who lunch," we really need to get together more often because you are all so inspiring.

Finally, thank you to the women I have met at Pelican Bay State Prison. So many of you shared your stories (on and off the record) and I have learned so much from you about love and limits, and love that knows no limits. Whenever the media talks about women in love with men in prison, it often portrays the women as fools. Perhaps all love is foolish, but I wanted to share how complex and challenging these relationships can be. Never in a million years did I expect to be part of this story, but then isn't life really what we thought would never happen in a million years?

My last thought: Thank you to the angel who brought me peace. I hope I can spread it around.

About the Author

Bridget Kinsella grew up at the New Jersey shore and attended Rutgers University and Columbia University's Graduate School of Journalism. She has been an editor with *Publishers Weekly* for fourteen years. When she's not visiting behind bars or buried in a book, she can be found racewalking near her home in northern California.